LISTEN TO THE VOICES, FOLLOW THE TRAILS

Discovering Maryland's Seaside Heritage

TOM PATTON

Copyright © 2005, Tom Patton

All Rights Reserved

No part of this book may be reproduced, stored in a retrieval system, or transmitted by any means, electronic, mechanical, photocopying, recording, or otherwise without written permission from the author.

ISBN: 0-9769347-3-6

Published by: Penned, Ink LLC
                Plainfield, IN 46168
                www.PennedInk.com

This publication has been funded in part by Worcester County Department of Tourism, Eastern Shore Rural Development Center, Lower Eastern Shore Heritage Council, Frazier Family Foundation, Quillin Foundation, and Berlin Heritage Foundation.

DEDICATION

The natural gifts and cultural heritage of Maryland's coastal bays are parts of a whole. Taken together, they form a certain Sense of Place that has indelibly characterized the region despite the impacts of contemporary land development. The organizations and individuals devoted to preserving these precious resources deserve our gratitude. Accordingly, all revenues from this publication will be donated to continuing stewardship of this coastal watershed.

Ode to the Coastal Bays

As if a swollen brain and nimble talk
endows only us with godly features,
we may fail to see on a morning's walk
all our ways in the lesser creatures.

Author

Cover Illustration:
Photo by Mike Gatty — www.dceventphotos.com.

TABLE OF CONTENTS

PREFACE vii

I. Exploration, Discovery and Preservation 1
II. Evolution of the Beaches, Bays, and Marshes:
    Tug-of-War Between Land and Sea 8
III. Nature's Resources and Scenic Treasures 26
IV. Assateague Indians and Early English Settlers:
    A Nearly Vanished Legacy 52
V. Colonial Architectural Gems:
    Imperiled Heritage Sites 70
VI. Barrier Island Settlements of the Past 89
VII. Seaside Legends, Yarns & Other Tales 104
    CONTEMPORARY VIEWS—IN COLOR—OF A FRAGILE HERITAGE 117
VIII. End of an Era, Two World Wars, and One Great Progger 127
IX. Bridges of Change..147
X. Assateague Island Offbeat Experiences 163
XI. Less-Traveled Byways along the Chincoteague Bay:
    Villages and Boat Landings Lost in Time 175
XII. Birding Adventures..195
XIII. A Solitary Outing: Reflections by a Once-Great Elm 207

Acknowledgements..219
Addendum: Some Eco "Dos and Don'ts": Excursion Ethics 221
Primary References..223
Additional Information 227

ECOGUIDE MAPS

Coastal Bays Watershed 7

Historic Milestones on Assateague Island 21-3

Heritage Sites: Sinepuxent & Newport Bays 88

Historic Berlin Walking Tour 162

Current Nature-Based Recreational Activities 174

Biking the Coastal Bays 188

Coastal Bays Kayak Trails 194

Birding & Boating the Coastal Bays 206

PREFACE

The genesis of this book came about several years ago on a fair, October Saturday marking National Estuary Day. Several of us were involved in leading an ecotour down the Sinepuxent Bay, sponsored by the Assateague Coastal Trust and celebrating the natural assets of Maryland's coastal waters. Tom Jones, Dean of Sciences and Technology at Salisbury University, gave the passengers an overview of how the coastal watershed was formed, and the craft's resident naturalist held a "show and tell" about some of the bay's critters that had been previously rounded up for such occasions. Alternating between the scientist and naturalist, my role was to point out some of the historic sites within view along the water's edge, toss in a few stories about people who had plied these waters over the centuries, and make a plea for historic preservation. After the cruise, Lee Whaley, U. S. Senator Paul Sarbanes's Eastern Shore representative, commented: "I've been on these trips before, but this is the first time that the environmental issues has been connected to the area's cultural heritage. It makes more sense."

What is the worth of stressing this Sense of Place—the distinctive heritage of a region in which we live or return to, time and again, to visit? Simply, this can be an image so indelible that it truly enriches our lives and creates moments of discovery and pure enchantment. When that special *it* begins to wane, so may the economic vitality and quality of life also suffer.

In my youth, just before the first half of the last century, I grew up on the then-secluded coastal bays of Maryland. Then was a glorious time before the influx of people, streams of tourists and boaters, developers, and all sorts of investors in the land. Why, a whole summer might be spent in bygone days on the bays without seeing more than a handful of work boats or fishing parties.

Older, I went out into the world to make a living, holding closely to those vivid memories. My life in faraway places made me even more sensitive to what was changing "back home": neighboring colonial properties that one by one were fading away; family farms turning into residential subdivisions; once-superb fishing and crabbing no longer to be taken for granted. More people using up the shrinking resources.

Along with the physical changes, the folk tales that had sprung out of the colorful past of stalwart watermen and rural farm life were fading from the language, withering on the thinning branches of native family trees. These are the people and their stories that I set out to capture. History is here, too, though as just enough backbone to hold together the "stuff" of oral history and the engaging struggle between our natural heritage and social development.

Yet, I do not believe the regional character has to give way entirely to change. My favorite places in the world—and probably yours, too—have managed to hold onto their traditional ways.

Listen to the Voices, Follow the Trails portrays the dynamic heritage that makes a day, or a lifetime, of excursions in the coastal bays watershed an exhilarating and thought-provoking experience. Each journey begins with a bird's-eye view (literally) of empty beaches, quiet water trails and rural back roads. Along the way, the memories of "old-timers" illuminate the trails. These are the dabs of color intended to catch a true reflection of time and place on a spare historical canvas. Just enough of the history to show how we are the way we are.

"Fish" Powell, perhaps the area's most visible citizen over the past fifty years, set the tone with his following recollections of the seaside during the past century:

REFLECTIONS ON A SEASIDE LIFE

Roland "Fish" Powell

Excerpts from the following conversation with the author in February 2005 capture a nostalgic view of the 20th century, based on "Fish's" unmatched experiences as: charter boat captain; businessman; Chief, Ocean City Fire Department; President, Ocean City Council; Mayor, Ocean City; President, Worcester County Commissioners; all-around outdoorsman; and friend to many.

I was born and raised here on Dorchester Street. This was a time when the streets were dirt, and water would trickle down the street on a good, high tide. We had no money, but I didn't know what the word "Depression" meant. We had something to eat in my family and we had a good place to sleep. No matter that the windows shook from a cold wind in the winter; we had one room with a little, wood-burning heater. In the summer we had the beach. When it got real hot, the floating shanties tied up at the end of the street could just pick up anchor and float down the bay—spend the summer clamming and fishing.

We could be mean little kids—always fighting—but no guns or knives or drugs or stuff like that. We were always hungry and we would go around to the back doors of the hotels and restaurants and ask if we could run any errands for them. Those days it was the women who ran most of these establishments, and they knew our families. Of course, they knew what we were there for and would whack us off slices from one of those good hams and maybe half a loaf of fresh, warm bread. Then, everything was fresh. We wanted to get to the pastries, too, and we would go up to the Royalton Hotel and see if we could work some sticky buns off of Miss Ethel Kelly.

On weekends, later on in high school, Art Davis and I would hike down to your parents' place on the bay and have a big old time playing in the water and eating your mom's cooking. Your mom was a great cook and would do her best to fill us up, but I don't know that she ever did. Those were the days!

When the inlet cut through in 1933 and the federal government came in to build the jetties and maintain it all, that gave a lot of local watermen a job. That was the first job that I can remember my father having, and he got some good money from it. During the winter months he also cooked or guided duck hunting parties down the bay to make a little bit of money.

Then the war came along (World War II), and fishing helped keep things going. You couldn't get gas for recreational fishing or to take out pleasure parties, but you could get all the gas you wanted for commercial fishing. And there were a lot more fish offshore, except for maybe blue fish, which, for whatever reason, were on a down trend. Maybe it was their scarcity; anyway, blue fish brought the highest price of any fish. I remember seeing a ticket at Davis & Lynch's fish dock paying 69 cents a pound for blue-fish. At the same time, flounder filets were selling in the market for 10 to 15 cents a pound. That's hard to believe now.

I went into the service at the end of World War II, and after I came out I ran one of Talbot Bunting's charter boats for ten years. That was the most enjoyment I ever had. One of my fishing parties was Felix Dupont. When he came on board, he brought his own captain, but as a fishing partner—that didn't bother me, because I was captain on my own boat. Felix Dupont could have almost owned his own navy, but he would come to Ocean City and fish with me.

One really pretty day in September we were running offshore and we were listening to all the charter boat captains chitchatting back and forth on their little shortwave sets: "Well, what are you going to do next week?" was the gist of it. One was going to put his boat up. Another one's going squirrel hunting. Another's got a Chesapeake retriever he wants to train. And another's got a pair of bird dogs he's going to start working out.

Well, Mr. Dupont's sitting there listening to all of that and he looks at me and says, "You know, you're the luckiest people in the world down here." I said, "Yeah, I guess so." He says, "You don't know what I'm talking about." I said, "Not really." I was 24 or 25 years old. He says, "I know some millionaires, but I'll be damned if I know anybody who lives more like millionaires than you people down here. You can have a little boat, own a dog, go gunning. The people I know would give anything in the world to be able to do what you guys take for granted. People I know own great big yachts with a captain running it—the owner has no idea how to run the boat or have that thrill of docking it or anything. Just to sit back on the fan tail of the boat with a drink in their hand and a blue sport coat on and a pair of white pants; that's what they think is living. Believe me, it's not." I've never forgotten that.

What really changed this area was, of course, the number of people who came here, and that was mostly with the building of the Chesapeake Bay Bridge. It got much easier for people to get here after that. Now everything needs to get stabilized. Government doesn't act as fast as private enterprise. You take the roads: your main roads are the same as they were 25 years ago. The infrastructure is lagging and the big, new builders who have moved in here are just covering everything with houses. The government can't cope with them that fast. Look at what's happening around Berlin and now down to Snow Hill, a sleepy village you might say. It's happening everywhere. All you have to do is fly into any airport at night and all you can see are solid lights up and down the whole East Coast.

When I was mayor I would hear people say, "Oh, here come these outsiders and they're going to do this and that." But you know, these are very active people and they serve on a lot of commissions. You would think they lived here for years because they have so much interest in things. They try to preserve more than the old natives. Of course, I can understand that. You take a native that's worked here all his life and never had a whole lot, didn't have a good paying job, then gradually the piece of property they had been living on, or maybe renting out a couple of rooms, became worth twice as much or twenty times more. This gave them the opportunity to live and enjoy what some of these other people who came here had enjoyed.

I've been around the world three times and I've never seen a nicer beach than here. It's the beach and the waters around it and what goes with it that draws the people…and as long as we have that, people are going to continue to come, for better or worse.

I

On a cold primeval night of the new moon
the long-eared owl slips out of the Island pines,
gliding quietly over life huddled in the wallow,
then stooping quickly to prey by a dim-lit path
leaving a shadow that sharp eyes might follow.

Exploration, Discovery, and Preservation

The weekenders come in a fast, steady stream down Route 50, out of Baltimore and Washington, eyes riveted straight ahead toward Ocean City. They could be wearing blinders, like harness race ponies at nearby Ocean Downs Raceway, protected against distractions on either side, right up to the finish line. Ah, the beach and the boardwalk and the smells of caramel popcorn, french fries, and pizza mixing with the salt air drifting off the ocean, as the road ends. It's a good finish...but not the one for this story.

With blinders removed, the visitors would have another view of Maryland's seaside that is ordinarily hidden just beyond their vision. And what they might enter here is a world hard to imagine within a few hours drive of two of the heaviest population centers in the United States. For here, as well as in the companion tidewater of the Eastern Shore of Virginia, is a still sparsely populated and naturally endowed region of historic village communities, wide-open stretches of sandy beach, largely untraveled rural byways, and lightly trafficked water trails in much of the coastal bays. However, it is noted at the outset, this idyllic picture is shrinking in size at a disturbing pace.

Making one's way off the beaten track to seek new experiences is the gist of the rapidly growing interest in heritage tourism—natural and cultural—which carries with it the bold message: "Learn about it, love it, and leave it no worse than before!" This nature-friendly trend, joined with an interlocking interest in historic sites, holds promise for balancing the scales between the forces of explosive population growth and protection of the natural and cultural treasures of the seaside. This traditional reference here to the "seaside" is used synonymously throughout, along with the more modern catch-all, "coastal bays."

Pressed against the Atlantic Ocean and largely isolated for centuries, the coastal bays watershed stretches narrowly along the entire length of Worcester County–Maryland's only window to the sea. Five contiguous coastal bays are embraced on the eastern side by popular ocean beaches and, to the west, a water-soaked drainage basin that reaches into the mainland for no more than an hour's hike on foot from the bays' edges. From north to south, these shallow coastal bays are designated as: the Assawoman and Isle of Wight Bays, lying behind Ocean City; the Sinepuxent Bay, immediately south of Ocean City and abreast of Assateague Island; Newport Bay, separated from the lower Sinepuxent Bay by a peninsula (Sinepuxent Neck); and, by far the largest, the Chincoteague Bay, extending behind Assateague Island into Virginia. These bays are laced with dozens of small "guts" and a few decent-sized tributaries that laze their ancient paths westward, away from the tidal currents of the main bays, and wind up, when left alone, at the damp feet of cotton bushes, bayberry, native holly, and pine thickets.

The place names of a number of the bays and historic sites are recognizable relics of local American Indian heritage. Derived loosely from an ancient Algonquian dialect and spelled phonetically, Assateague has been commonly translated as "The Place Across." However, other translations of Assateague vary, as is often the case with archaic, spoken-only languages. Assateague may also have meant "Long Low Yellow-Brown River of Sand Across the Water" or possibly "Fast-running Stream Between." Similar variations occur with Sinepuxent, although the consensus is for "Stony (or possibly, shell-filled), Watery Swamp." Assawoman (Bay) may not mean anything as anatomical as it appears; one translation has it as a "Shallow Cave in the Water." Chincoteague may be simpler: "Large Stream and Inlet." In any case, one word in the local native dialect can be packed with flowery imagery.

Today, the five coastal bays and adjoining beaches are the destination of ten million visitors annually. While a good percentage of these visits involve a degree of outdoor activity, there is much more outside the mainstream of ocean bathing, sun-tanning, and fishing that remains largely untapped. After the bathers have fled the beaches and flounder fishermen have stowed their rods, other pursuits are waiting. Bird watchers are attracted year-around by some 360 species of shorebirds, songbirds, raptors, and waterfowl, some of which are now uncommon at best or, at worst, threatened or endangered species. The climate is temperate; there is no closed season on canoeing, kayaking, beachcombing, hiking, and biking.

Ecotourism is also allied with interests in the social fabric of the community. Visitors may search out the noteworthy colonial homes and the charm of historic settlements such as Berlin and Snow Hill. Country inns and B&Bs, local artists, crafts, antique shops, fresh seafood from the local waters, and friendly Main Streets complete the picture.

By no means is this account to be taken as a Chamber of Commerce promotion; rather, the attitude here is "come if you must" and enjoy it, if you will, on certain terms. Nor will the reader find every last detail on water trails, hiking and biking paths, or historic sites. Specific brochures are available to serve those with more particular interests. However, here is a fair start for any number of activities that beckon from the countryside.

The narrative also comprises this writer's selective view of local history—a lifetime of experiences along the coastal bays, and the desire to get certain recollections into print before all is forgotten and the reference points have been lost to a new generation. These highlights are intended to catch the flavor of the dish, without laying out the whole meal: that is, enough to aid in the discovery of a Sense of Place—the very essence of this coastal destination that instinctively draws us to it, the character we wish to preserve.

These observations are also intended to bring certain questions to mind. How did this beach, island, or marsh develop? Is it growing, shrinking, sinking? What is the current health of the bays? Tell about that old brick house standing vacantly beside the water's edge. What distinguished the people who settled the area? Or, where can one go and find one's own space to get away from it all? The questions, loose as they may appear, are related. They are meant to encourage a look around from a new perspective, accompanied by a growing feeling of stewardship.

The travels down these trails may be thought of as a modern-day exploration. The goal may not be as lofty as the long-ago search for a shortcut to the distant lands of the spice trade by such explorers as Giovanni da Verrazano, perhaps the first European to touch upon the Maryland seaside nearly 500 years ago. Yet, the process of discovering the special nature of the region can be a true adventure, an "authentic" experience. This usually requires some thoughtful digging beneath the surface impressions. An archaeologist goes through a similar exploration in piecing together a past civilization from a few old bones, projectile points, chipped relics, or the fragile structure of a colonial home. Likewise, getting the full picture of the coastal bays brings into play a certain detective work: as the pieces of natural and cultural history are put together and the dots connected, the appreciation multiplies and questions are answered. Time after time, what one often discovers is the influence of geography on human development—and vice-versa.

This chronicle may be read, too, as a story that proceeds more or less from the dawn of the last Ice Age to the present day—with each era leaving an imprint on all that follows. Events portray a typical pattern of change along much of the country's coastline. First, we behold a desolate coastal frontier, which early European settlers wrested from Stone Age Indians, then moved on to colonize our inland cities. Now, in reverse, the urban colonizers are returning in droves to the edges of the sea. Although much of these current visitations are centered on Ocean City and the "upper" coastal bays, this chronicle takes the less-traveled paths through the watershed, where there is much else to savor.

Throughout this narrative journey, one finds people who have left their imprints behind, especially by way of their reflective and, occasionally, wistful voices. These have been recorded for posterity, as fragments of our oral history, by the National Park Service (NPS), Taylor House Museum (THM), and this writer (TP). (The initials will be used to identify the sources of the abridged histories included later.) The voices resonate with a native dialect and inflection that have long tested the ear of "outsiders." The echoes add much to the experience of passing along a wooded trail, of navigating an otherwise quiet stretch of water, or contemplating the remains of a once-elegant colonial brick home.

A characteristic voice was that of George Bertrand Cropper (1908-2005), a formidable figure in the development of Ocean City during the twentieth century. Among his many stories, the memories of World War II serve to remind that this was a pivotal turn in local history—when families realized, often for the first time, that there was another world away from the seaside...and once exposed to it, an enduring isolation would begin to dissolve.

Bert Cropper (THM: 1995)

Well, in 1939, we had been reading about the trouble with Hitler and the English sending the Prime Minister (Neville Chamberlain) over there. I remember very well (Chamberlain) coming back and saying we have peace in our time. But for some reason or other the reaction here was that Chamberlain was a weak sissy. Hitler had gotten pretty close to Mussolini , and we were also apprehensive about Russia and Mussolini signing this compact with Germany. When (Hitler) did invade Poland, the rapidity in which Poland fell really impressed us all very seriously. Then when the Germans invaded France, it actually fell within a couple of weeks. Here was this big country with 2,000,000 men standing army...here they had built the Maginot line, but Hitler had

> come around the end of it through Belgium. And we didn't realize that their tanks were so wonderful, much further ahead of our own tanks.
>
> Early in the war, I remember very well one of our freighters was sunk off Ocean City, and the Coast Guard had brought all these bodies back. I asked Jack (John Whaley, Ocean City Ice Plant owner), who was my next-door neighbor, could I go down and help ice them up. I went down and came back the next day and went and volunteered for the service. I was curious about World War I and I would ask all these fellows who had been in the war and those hadn't been in the war, and it impressed me that those that hadn't gone in the war had a great big excuse why they didn't go. I don't know if that had any effect on my decision to volunteer or not, but I guess I wanted to be in the war.

Such voices are often our only real guide, the truest connection to our heritage.

Coastal Bays Watershed

Isolated by natural barriers for nearly all of its 10,000 years of human settlement, the coastal bays watershed features an uncommon ecological and social development that has been generally spared from external forces until after World War II.

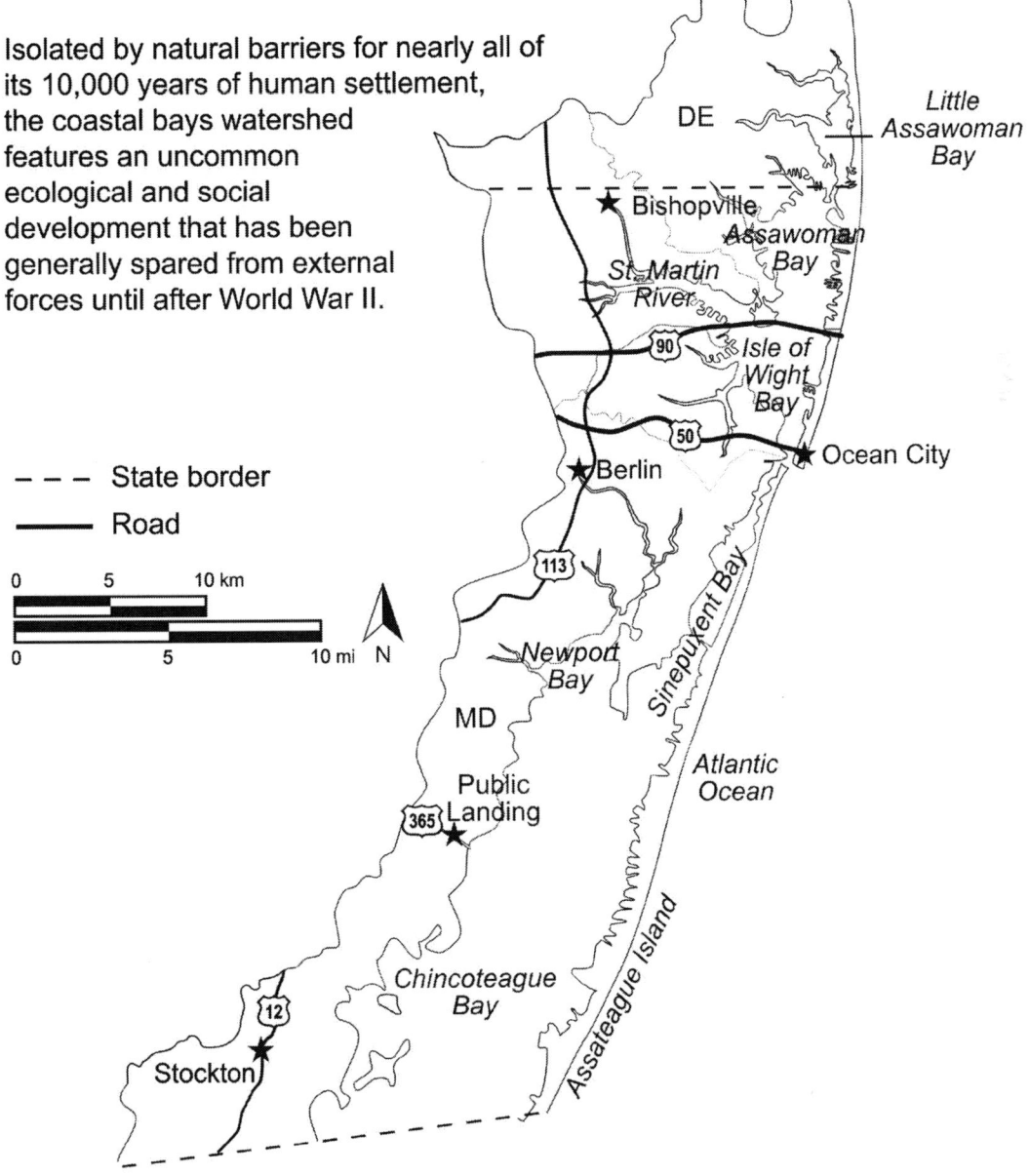

II

Soaring on an updraft high above the land
the bald eagle eyes the far rim of the sea,
then pitches on a stretch of barren sand,
and is surprised to find, side by side ,
a horseshoe crab and a concrete slab.

Evolution of the Beaches, Bays, and Marshes: Tug of War between Land and Sea, Man and Nature

Imagine a low-throttled boat ride down the Sinepuxent Bay. The craft begins to draw away from the throngs on the beach at Ocean City and the congestion of boats converging and dispersing at the head of the Ocean City Inlet. The summer morning lies calmly on the water. It is still early and the southerly trade winds have yet to freshen. Bait fish skip ahead on the surface, rising above flashing predators underneath snapper bluefish. Gulls cry overhead. The boat moves well with the incoming tide, as the current eddies in a line away from the channel markers down the bay. Slowly, the early traffic of fishermen thins, and the view begins to focus on the quieter waters and landscapes that give a picture of the watershed as it has long existed, and as it continues to play a role in the local life-style.

Here is a short primer on the interplay of geological, ecological, and cultural forces at work in Maryland's seaside; for in this most narrow section of the coastal bays, the elements are tightly compressed for easy viewing and interpretation. Some basic facts, reduced to a digestible minimum, are the building blocks to understanding other features of the region's environmental and cultural heritage.

The distance between Assateague Island and the marsh-fringed mainland shore is less than a mile. The enduring impacts of storms, sea-level rise, and shoreline change are readily apparent. Nature's living resources are at hand to be pursued, harvested, or simply appreciated for what they are. The Sinepuxent Bay may be seen, too, as a telling middle-ground between the more developed and populated "upper" bays behind Ocean City and the lightly explored regions of the "lower" bays. The visitor can both appreciate the past and glimpse what the future may hold.

The distinctive quirks of natural history start here, with an overview of the rapid geographic evolution occurring since the end of the last Ice Age. In just 10,000 years, a mere blink of the eye in geologic time, the silt from melting glaciers has spilled out of the Delaware River basin and other coastal drainage systems to help form the barrier island's sandy beaches, shallow coastal bays, and broad tidal marshes. Until recently, this evolving watershed remained isolated from the rest of the Delmarva Peninsula and points farther west. Dense, inland forests and the impenetrable swamps of the Pocomoke River kept away both friend and foe—until paved roads connected across the Eastern Shore and over the Chesapeake Bay Bridge a half-century ago. A sense of "apartness" remained ingrained in the local character ever since the first Native American Indians set down their encampments.

The natural confinement of the coastal bays watershed may convey certain ecological advantages when compared to the far more expansive and environmentally-challenged watershed of the Chesapeake Bay. Most of the rain that falls out of the sky over the Delmarva Peninsula runs off fertilized lawns and the tarred surfaces, or roads and driveways, while also carrying farm-site nutrients out through the cross-stitching of drainage ditches and tributaries that eventually flow into the Chesapeake Bay. However, size can be a two-edged sword: fewer pollutants can be just as harmful as they collect in the shallow, slow-flushing coastal bays. In any case, this constant interplay of natural and man-made forces continues to define land-use issues that have been fought over for more than 300 years. As the local population grows, so does the gravity of the problem.

Perhaps even more than the impacts of centuries of coastal storms, powerful ocean currents, and recent land development, it is the slow-moving change in sea levels that may be dictating the evolutionary process. As the glaciers melted, the seas began to rise, fairly rapidly at first, then slowing to about an inch per century by the 1800s. However, the ocean and tidal estuaries are now rising more quickly again—1-2 inches per decade, or more than a foot per century. This quickening pace of sea-level rise has been correlated to global warming. According to a bulletin from the U. S. Environmental Protection Agency (June 2001), average temperature in the region has risen 1 degree Fahrenheit over the last century. This rise is expected to continue over the next century to possibly as high as 10 degrees over the current norm. However, there is another theory proposed by some scientists that speculates a cooling trend in the future, as ice floes break away from the Arctic and Antarctic glaciers and move among warmer currents toward the equator.

Either way, the melting ice is likely to accelerate the rate of sea level rise and, if only in the distant future, increase inundation of the barrier island, wetlands, and mainland settlements. The longer-term potential for massive impact on property development at the water's edge is obvious. We already see the future in ever-higher flood tides, in the islands and smaller, marshy tumps that are sinking below the surface of the bays, and in the front yards of homes, no longer standing untouched above the surge of storm waters.

In effect, the physical appearance of the coastline, as well as the entire ecosystem, could change dramatically in just a few generations, or even with one cataclysmic thrust. The threat of such changes should reasonably dictate how and where land development takes place in the future.

Evolution of the Beaches, Bays, and Marshes

That the coastline has changed significantly since the Ice Age is revealed on Assateague Island. As land masses gradually submerged under the rising ocean, the edge of the sea moved some fifty miles or more inland from the continental shelf to its present barrier island location. The westward drift of Assateague Island and encroachment of the seas are visible on a very low "spring," or lunar, tide, when the synergistic positions of sun and moon cause abnormal tidal fluctuations. Dark stumps of long-submerged pine and cedar trees rise briefly, ghost-like, in the surf and then subside once again below the foam of breaking waves.

Where will the next high-water mark stop, one may wonder. It may be well to consider that present seawater levels have yet to reach even a halfway point in the periodic westward thrusts that start at the precipice of the ocean canyons, fifty miles or more off today's shoreline, and move inexorably toward the Appalachian Mountains. In the last epochal encroachment, the sea eventually stopped on the up-slope of the Piedmont Plateau, where remains of millennia-old oyster shells signify the earlier high-water mark.

Larry Smack, a.ka. Chief Medicine Cat (TP: 2004)

I'm 72 years old now, so when I used to come onto Assateague when I was young, that was a long time ago; long before the bridge over to the island, even before the war. And it was quite a bit different then, especially on the north end. The biggest thing then maybe was there used to be so much more vegetation, the beach was a lot wider and it had humongous dunes. That was when they still had cows over there. I know, because they got after me one time. When you think about it, the Island hadn't changed much since my ancestors (Native Americans) camped there and that can go back as far as you want, yes, thousands of years. When the white man moved in here, we didn't own the land, didn't own the island. "I'll give you this box of trinkets, if you'll move off the land," he said. And now you look at it and it's hard to imagine that all these changes have happened since then. I'll tell you something later about being visited by the Spirit

> **when I went through a time of healing myself on Assateague, and having a vision of my ancestors. I'll tell you my story, in a bit, of following the Native Path.**

As the mainland receded into the sea during the present geologic age, Assateague Island, like other barrier islands along the Atlantic coast, emerged over 6,000 years ago from the transported sediment. Rising above normal high tides, the barriers of sand would trap seawater between beach and mainland to form lagoon-like coastal bays. Adding to the historic deposits of sediment, a prevailing north-to-south ocean current sweeps from New England down through the Mid-Atlantic Bight (the recessed coastline from New Jersey to North Carolina), assisting in the dispersal of granular particles from the ocean bed. Although in-shore eddies of current may move in either direction, it appears that sands along the coast at Cape Henlopen and Rehoboth Beach, Delaware, eventually migrate along the Maryland beaches. Delaware's loss is possibly Maryland's gain, however briefly, when nor'easters buffet the coast and huge waves roil and rake out sand from under vacation homes in Dewey Beach and Bethany Beach, followed by fresh deposits of sand on the Maryland shores. Then, in a continuum, Maryland's loss of sand may become Virginia's gain—and so on down the coast.

Like other coastal barrier islands, Assateague Island is slowly shifting and rolling westward as the sea rises. Other notable changes over time have occurred with the opening and closing of inlets, usually opening with the powerful bore of a hurricane or nor'easter that pushes the ocean over the beach, slicing gullies through the sand and flooding the bay. This event may then be followed immediately by the backlash of a strong northwest wind, which pushes the flood water back out to sea and further deepens the gully into a full-scale inlet. Eventually the inlet closes, this time more slowly, if nature is left to its own devices.

At least eleven such inlets have been counted since the English settlers came to these shores, though only two are open today—at Ocean City and Chincoteague. One of the closed inlets, Sinepuxent Inlet, stayed open abreast of South Point for an unusually long 82 years (1735-1817) and figured prominently in colonial history as the primary entrance for sea-going ships into the coastal bays. Traces of the former inlets may be detected in the flat, shell-strewn zones on the island and by the bay-side shoals, now covered in salt marsh. A particular clue to the location of Sinepuxent Inlet is the deposit of ships' ballast stones lying on the bottom of the bay in a line between the tip of South Point and Assateague Island. Here, trading ships unloaded their ballast upon clearing the inlet and prior to coming to port, usually at Newport Landing. The ballast on outgoing vessels would then comprise new cargoes of lumber, grain, and tobacco.

Over time, inlets have also defined the length of Assateague Island as well as its various location names. Until the legendary 1933 Hurricane, which created the Ocean City Inlet, Assateague and Fenwick Islands were merged as one continuous shoreline. A seven-mile portion of the island, extending from just south of Ocean City to the Sinepuxent Inlet, was called North Beach—meaning north of this inlet. A portion of beach below this former inlet was referred to as South Beach. Though these designations are now spoken of by only a few old-timers, they are used in this text as convenient descriptions to describe historic events.

The Historical Base Map, prepared by the National Park Service, depicts a number of such natural and human developments on the island. The map is also useful in understanding how the island—once privately owned—is now divided among various government authorities. Established by an Act of Congress in 1965, the Assateague Island National Seashore extends from Ocean City, Maryland, to the Maryland-Virginia state line, and covers an area of over 48,000 acres—of which, approximately 17,000 are terrestrial and 31,000 aquatic. The National Park Service also assists the U.S. Fish and Wildlife Service in the management of the Toms Cove Hook portion of the Chincoteague National Wildlife Refuge on the Virginia portion of the island. The Chincoteague Refuge had already been authorized in 1943, and its 9,000 acres continues to serve the purpose of wildlife protection for which it was originally established. The Assateague (Maryland) State Park was established in the same time frame as the National Park and covers a little more than 750 acres, beginning just north of the Verrazano Bridge and extending two miles southward. The Verrazano Bridge was constructed in 1963 to provide easy access from the mainland in anticipation of private, commercial development of the island. Soon after, both federal and state agencies secured a gateway around the base of the bridge on the mainland side, including locations for the Barrier Island Visitor Center (federal) and a recreational pier and boat launch (state).

Preserving Assateague Island
Ilia Fehrer, Conservationist (NPS: 2004)

I don't know if you know Judy Johnson. She has been my mentor. As the head of the Committee to Preserve Assateague Island, she did a tremendous job, and I really can't take the credit for it. I was working with her because she needed eyes and ears locally, but she had so many contacts with the federal government and with a lot of the other national conservation organizations.

Well, she and her son came down to Assateague (from Baltimore) and camped there. Of course, in the early days there was very little there. No infrastructure. None of the park as we know it now. But she fell in love with Assateague and just thought it was the most glorious place in the world and should be protected for everybody to enjoy the pristine qualities of an undeveloped wild beach. Even the preservation of some little endangered grasses and species were important to her. She was a thorn in the side of the Superintendents of Assateague, I'll tell you. She just watched them. She was down here almost every weekend with her little camper, and she knew everything that was happening on Assateague.

Then when the legislation had been passed to approve Assateague as a National Seashore, a part of that legislation called for a road connecting the north end of Assateague to Chincoteague (allowing some commercial development). We went to Congress to testify in Washington in opposition to that road...and we were beginning to realize how ephemeral Assateague is, that it continues to move. Sand is washing

> westward all the time as the sea level rises, and a road would not be a very good investment. Anyway, we had that part of the legislation approving Assateague deleted.
>
> There was a lingering resentment, though, about Assateague National Seashore because a lot of people had bought up lots on Assateague. And a lot of people saw Assateague as another Ocean City where they could make a lot of money and sell lots and real estate. The real estate people in Worcester County were for a long time really chagrined... maybe a few are still that way.

While it took thousands of years for the ocean currents and sea-level rise to form this dune-studded island, it has taken less than half a century for several severe storms to reduce North Beach to little more than a high sandbar. This is the view we may see on the port side during the seven-mile boat ride down the Sinepuxent Bay from West Ocean City to the Verrazano Bridge.

It is hard to imagine that as late as midway in the last century majestic, primary dunes were common on North Beach and supported a full cover of dune grasses and plentiful sand-trapping vegetation; and along the bayside of the island, a maze of lush marshes and intertwining sloughs still provided splendid wildlife habitat. The reason for the accelerated pattern of westward migration and erosion of the beach has been the seaward protrusion of stone jetties at the Ocean City Inlet. Constructed after a natural passage was opened through the beach during the 1933 Hurricane, the inlet structure has blocked the normal drift of sand south of the jetty—in effect, starving North Beach of its natural replenishment. The "perfect storm" of January 1992, a monster of a nor'easter that formed as two major low-pressure fronts joined near Assateague Island, completed the damage. A huge surge of sea toppled across North Beach, erasing dunes, suffocating the marsh with sediment, filling in the sloughs, and ripping out shrubs and small trees that normally stemmed the wear and tear of erosion.

Fortunately, there have been few major coastal storms over the past few years, and vegetation is beginning to return to North Beach. A federal project to restore this portion of the beach is now helping maintain the integrity of this north end, as it continues to retreat in a westward flow.

Island Sink Holes
Nat Steelman (NPS: 1971)

...Not too far above there (Pope Island) is where Pope's Island Ditch goes almost to the ocean. We hear tell of quicksand and wonderin' why it's quicksand. My father always claimed there were springs underground, which make for sure 'nough quicksand, and that's enough reason. He always cautioned me: "Be careful, Son. Watch how you step out when you get to the end of this thoroughfare on the beach, where the sand is, because there are springs there and there is no bottom." He says I have taken long poles and tried, (but) I never found where it would bring up; naturally a person would sink right down. Now in modern times I think I have learned why. It's supposed to be a tremendous underground fresh water river coming from above Salisbury....It also goes down similar to Delaware Bay or the Chesapeake, and it seems it has a downward movement with its offshore movement. It goes under the Pocomoke. It also comes to this very place my father was speaking about where this quicksand was. Now as time goes on, surfaces shift. Maybe it'll harden one place, but it'll soften another. Two or three years ago we had a tremendous run of rock (fish) here. Airplane pilots told me that there was a difference in the color of the water, showin' that fresh water was flowin' in the ocean from off of this very spot, and we knew that rock fish congregate where the fresh water was.

A relatively recent feature of the island is the rounded hook on the south end in Virginia, adjacent to the island community of Chincoteague. The hook, like a moving set of jaws, has formed over the course of the past century as a result of the continuing deposits of sand from storm, wind, and tide. As it encloses, the jaw tightens around Tom's Cove, once the location of the choicest wild-growing Chincoteague oysters. Although the natural oysters have virtually disappeared—largely depleted by predators, viral pathogens, and over-harvesting—a thriving shellfish aquaculture business has emerged in its place.

Nat Steelman, cont'd.

I have my own thoughts about MSX (virus affecting oysters). I'm not a laboratory man, but I think it's truly like you put prisoners in a concentration camp and don't give 'em enough food and maybe they'll develop 'berculosis or somethin' else. I think this is the case of the arster (oyster) bein' 'round his natural environment, for what he would eat to keep hisself goin'. The plankton, such as we would have, is a shortage of it, and I think it makes the arster turn queer. I'm afraid that civilization is progress in one sense, but with an arster it's anything but progress. He needs to be where it's wild, where he has some rest from oils and chemicals, and a good drainage of food to him. I think MSX would take care of itself if (the arster) could be more in his natural environment like he originally had.

Viewing the island as a whole, the topographic differences that occur from north to south are significant. Toward the south end, Assateague Island becomes wider, with greater contour. The higher elevations and better soils are just enough to support more luxuriant vegetation and, once upon a time, human settlements. Freshwater ponds, formerly dotting the entire length, are now located south of the Verrazano Bridge. The ponds are "sink holes" in the island where groundwater rises to the surface. The oases that formed about these ponds have been lost to the erosion on North Beach during the past half-century, but still provide watering holes for wildlife elsewhere on the Island.

Shifting our view to the waters on all sides, what may be noticed at first glance is the extreme shallowness of the bays. The average depth is less than four feet and has been decreasing continually over the years from wind- and tide-borne sedimentation. Numerous sandbars often infringe upon the main channel and serve as efficient hazards to navigation. Generally, the coastal bays are even shallower, with sandier bottoms, on the eastern side, behind Assateague Island. This is largely attributable to the deposits of sand that wash off the beach during severe storms and high tides.

The lack of depth, poor flushing, and extreme shifts in water temperature through the seasons contribute to a fragile ecosystem. To put this in perspective, the entire volume of water in Maryland's coastal bays is not much more than that of the Choptank River—the latter being only one of numerous tributaries flowing into the Chesapeake Bay. Hence, even small changes in the coastal ecology can be quickly magnified throughout the system. In summer, as temperatures rise, these shallow bays become saltier, with diminished oxygen levels. This adds to the stress on a number of underwater creatures. Nonetheless, the bays—with their extensive habitat of submerged aquatic vegetation (SAV)—remain a productive nursery for commercially important finfish and shellfish. Current efforts to protect the SAV in the coastal bays from the impacts of hydraulic clam-dredging, boat propeller scarring, and nutrient runoff, among other factors, seem to be having positive results.

Throughout the coastal bays are a number of small islands, most being no more than an acre or so in size, that have come about from both natural and man-made forces. The natural islands, usually the larger with heavier vegetation, tend to lie close to the shoreline on either side of the bays. Quite likely, some of these islands were once attached to either the barrier island or mainland, but later separated and began the process of shrinking and submerging into the bays as a result of erosion and rising sea levels.

Other islands, usually located near the main channel, are sometimes referred to as "spoil" islands, since the material that composes these islands was pumped to the island sites when the channel was dredged during the 1930s in an unsuccessful effort to connect the coastal bays to the Intracoastal Inland Waterway. Much controversy has been attached in recent years to federal plans for redredging south of Ocean City, and the channel has been left in the meantime to fill in as nature directs. But whatever the environmental pluses or minuses of deepening the main channel and creating spoil islands, these spoil sites have provided exceptional nesting habitats for a variety of shorebirds. An example of a spoil island can be seen in Sinepuxent Bay just north of Snug Harbor, and another just below the Verrazano Bridge. They are worth viewing from their shorelines for their abundant populations of wading birds. However, it is advised not to disturb the interior of the islands during the nesting season, which generally coincides with the spring and summer tourist season. Even if the islands are not posted at this time, skydiving terns may give the invader second thoughts.

Not too many years ago, the general view of the tidal marshlands along the bays was "not in my front yard" unless covered over with fill-dirt, paved, and finished in front with creosote and arsenic-treated wooden bulkheads or stone riprap. Such was the aim of getting rid of the muck and that low-tide smell of methane, or marsh gas, arising from the natural decomposition of organic matter. But recently we have learned much more about the enormous economic and ecological benefits of salt marshes, with their rich detritus of decayed tidal grasses. Acre for acre, these marshes—churning with living organisms—may be the most productive protein factories on the planet. At the base of a complex food chain, the marshes feed the marine life of much of the entire ocean. The loss of each little patch of these fertile food machines ends up starving an expanse of the sea itself.

Marshes also stabilize shorelines and aid in flood control. They maintain water quality as a natural filtration system by straining off pollutants such as pesticides, nitrates, and toxic wastes. Instrumental in the system of filtering runoff and supplying beneficial nutrients are two species of spartina grasses: *Spartina patens*, the hardy high-marsh cordgrass, or salt meadow hay, which stands barely above the normal tide; and *Spartina alterniflora*, the low-marsh, salt cordgrass that thrives along the regularly flooded edges of the bays. Especially important to marine life, these tidal marshes are the incubators of an array of living resources, including fish, shellfish, waterfowl, shorebirds, and terrestrial wildlife. The spartina grasses, too, have been the fodder that for centuries fed the wild horses of Assateague and the grazing livestock of the early European settlers.

Marsh grasses play a role in a number of stories about the delicate balance of nature. One intriguing interaction involves a partnership of spartina with the snail-like marsh periwinkle and the native blue crab. The periwinkle feeds on spartina and is fed upon by the crab. In times, when crab populations are low, the numbers of periwinkles explode and ravish the marsh grasses. In turn, the loss of marsh-producing protein starves a wide-flung maritime dependency. Such is the fragility of this tidal ecosystem.

The marshes, bays, and beaches formed as a trio of closely linked geologic forces, evolving in a harmony that includes the dissonant notes of acute natural events and the interventions of man. It's all part of the barrier island story. Storm-created inlets, rising sea levels, beach erosion, man-made canals through the marsh, and bulkhead construction are just a few of the changes that are visible to boaters making their way down the bay. Hurricanes and rise in sea level we cannot stop. Waterfront development and construction practices that result in loss of marshes and marine habitat may be manageable.

To this end, the Atlantic Coastal Bays Critical Area Program has been established to help manage development within 1,000 feet of the tidal wetlands and to provide for a natural, vegetated buffer along a 100-foot-wide zone next to the tidal edge. Protection of this shoreline buffer—with its capacity to filter runoff, stabilize shorelines, and provide a refuge for intertidal wildlife—is the centerpiece of Critical Area Law.

The swings of the pendulum between the sanctity of private property rights versus management of natural resources for the public good began on the seaside with the first clash between European and Native American. The debate continues in the present era, and its reverberations rise above the hum of the engine as this excursion navigates down the bays and the view to starboard fills with new construction.

Historic Milestones on Assateague Island
Top Section

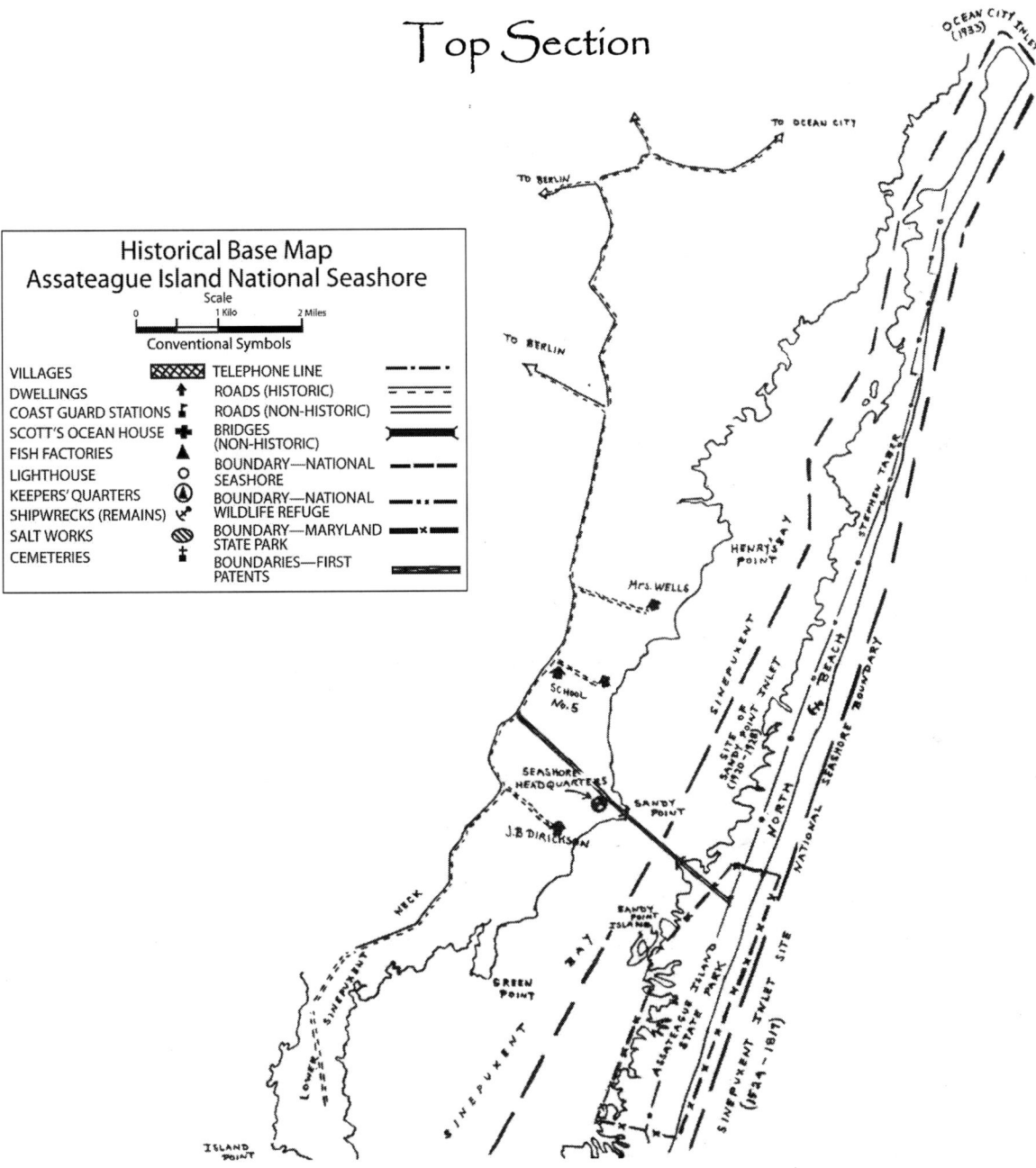

Prepared by the National Park Service in 1968, the "General Background and Historical Base Map" documents outstanding features of Assateague Island, as well as changes made over the past 300 years. Although some of the sites no longer exist, or have been much altered over time, these nonetheless provide a basis for appreciating the remarkable story of this barrier island.

Middle Section

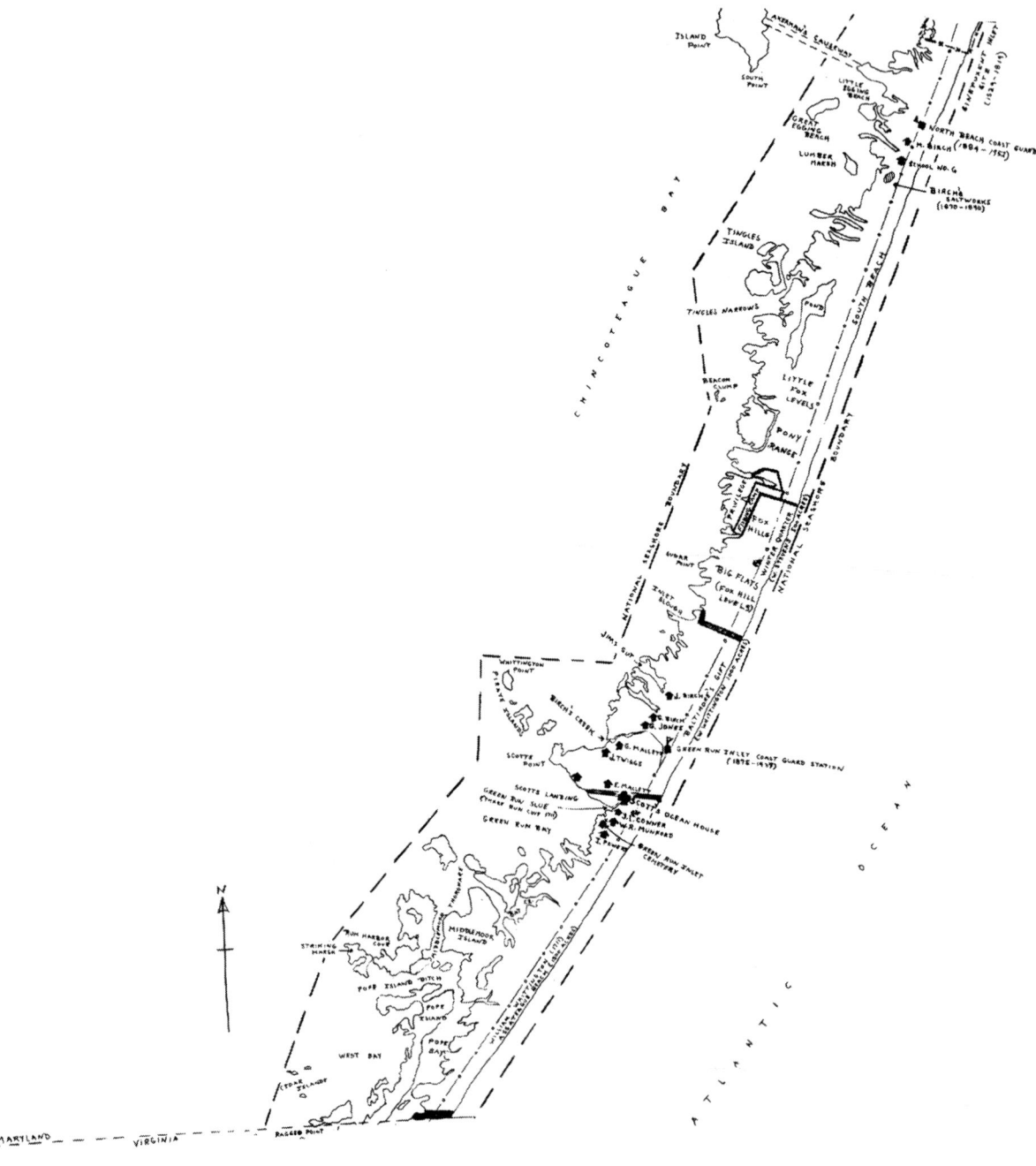

This section begins just above "Akerman's Causeway," a local term sometimes used to describe the ferry-crossing between South Point and Assateague. During the 1950s, Akerman and his real estate sales agents shared the ferry with duck hunters and a declining number of seasonal residents on the island.

Bottom Section

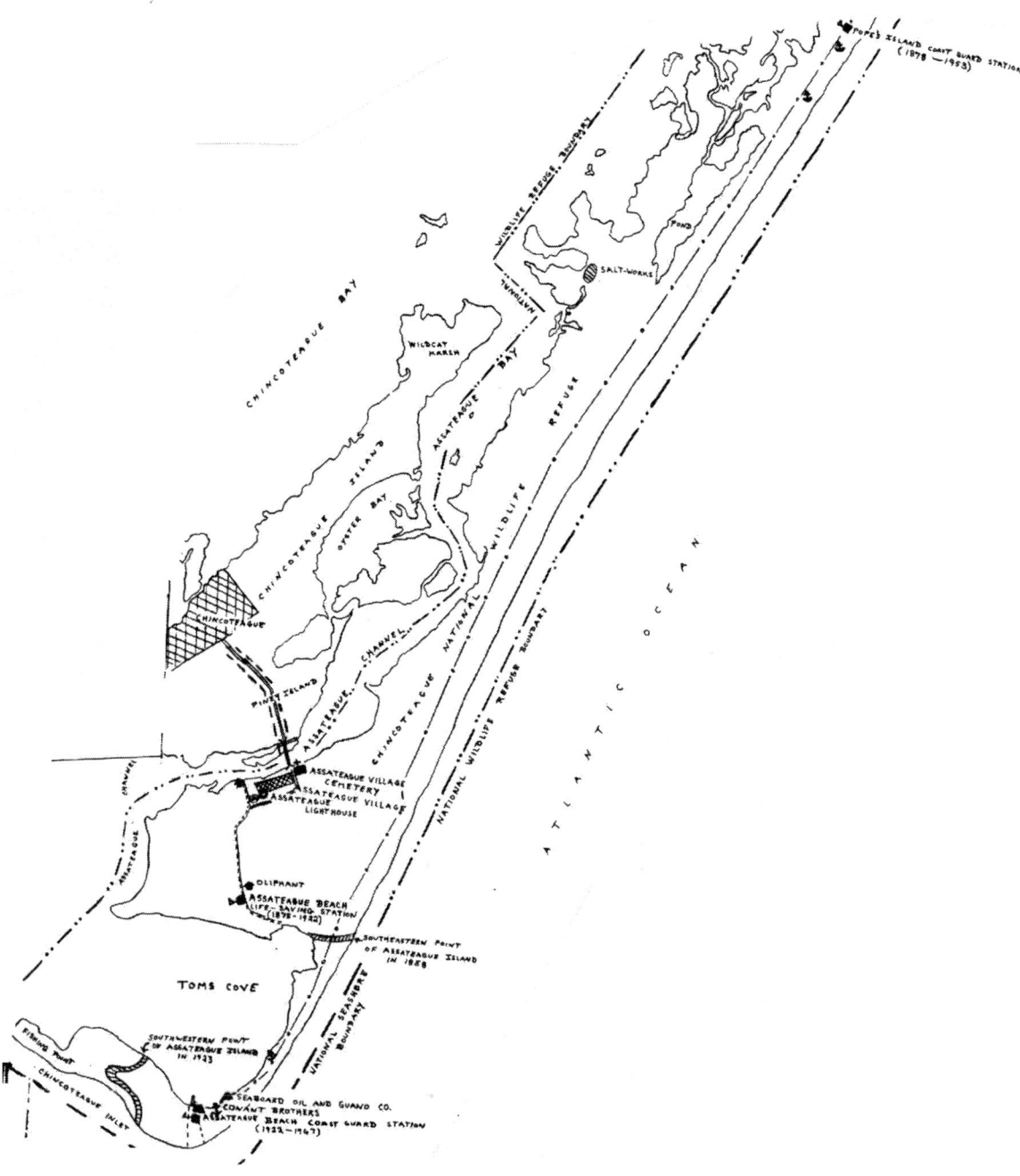

This section is now taken up by the Chincoteague Wildlife Refuge. Physical changes have added to the southern tip over the past century, creating Tom's Cove in the process. The gain of sand on the south end of barrier islands, aided by ocean currents, is a typical pattern along the Atlantic coast.

Some changes take a millennium...some less than a day

Above, on a very low tide, the stumps of a former pine forest are briefly exposed in the surf on Assateague Island. The former woodlands once extended to the continental shelf, roughly forty miles eastward beyond the current edge of the sea. The advance of the ocean has been ongoing since the end of the last Ice Age.

Below, during the January 1992 nor'easter, catastrophic flooding swept over much of the island and well into the mainland. The north end of the island migrated several hundred yards eastward—flattened and scoured of vegetation.

Photos courtesy of National Park Service

The 1933 Hurricane

On August 20, 1933, the rain began to fall. A nor'easter made its appearance on the seaside, waiting to be joined by the most destructive tropical storm to hit this coast in the 20th century.

Over the course of 72 hours, the two colliding storms would dramatically change the natural and social development of the region. The boardwalk, hotels, and cottages of Ocean City were largely obliterated. Fishermen's camps at the south end of town were demolished. Yet the property losses would soon be recovered many times over by the creation of the Ocean City Inlet. A new offshore and sportfishing industry was born. Only a year prior to the storm, an estimated 5,000 vacationers visited the Maryland seaside. Then years later, the number would increase to 100,000 annual visits. In another half-century, the figure would reach 10,000,000.

Photo courtesy of National Park Service

III

From distant poles and places undone
they may return if left alone;
the osprey in March to last year's nest,
and piping plover, curlew , and dunlin,
an even chance to stop and rest.

Nature's Resources and Scenic Treasures

Game-filled forests, bays teeming with fish and shellfish, and skies clouded with waterfowl marked this long-isolated tidewater region as a food-gathering paradise for the Assateague Indians. Hides of the since-vanished black bear, timber wolves, elk, cougar, and bobcat clothed the Assateagues and, together with other still-common fur-bearers, provided the initial means of trade between Indian and European during the so-called "Contact" period of the seventeenth century. Sea-salty oysters, clams, and fish were readily at hand—taken easily as a natural right by the Native Americans, then by European settlers, and now, in diminished quantities, by commercial watermen and recreational hunters and fishermen. The varying abundance of fish and game has affected social history at every turn. Today, the tourism-based economy and the commercial fisheries warily compete for shares of this natural resource.

Diminishing populations of many species of wildlife have given rise to a greater concern for conservation. A new ethic is emerging. The hunter with a gun is now sharing time with those shooting with a camera. Catching unlimited numbers of fish is giving way to fishing under stricter "catch limits," or for sport-only. Taking fish and game from the wild without "giving something back" is now being supplemented with commercial aquaculture and game farming. Although this author still counts himself among the endangered species of food-gatherers, the images that stay fixed in memory have far less to do with the hunter's "bag" than with quiet moments of observation and reflection.

It's now time to visit a few natural features of the mainland shore—with care not to trespass on private property without the owner's permission.

Along the edge of the marsh are clumps of the plentiful ribbed mussel, which help stabilize the marsh bank on both sides of the bays against erosion. Mussels also feed the small, four-legged marsh-prowlers: raccoons, opossums, and the increasingly plentiful river otters. Although not as esteemed in the kitchen as the blue mussel found elsewhere, the ribbed mussel is edible and has fed many hungry campers. Farther along, the marsh yields squadrons of fiddler crabs, which scurry away from approaching footsteps like so many frantic vacationers fleeing the beach in advance of an approaching storm.

Upon the approach of intruders, blue crabs and bullhead minnows become active, stirring up the muddy bottoms of man-made mosquito ditches. Although well-intended to help drain mosquito-breeding tidal pools, the ditches have altered the marsh habitat—as many feel, to the general detriment of wildlife. However, as the ditches have begun to fill in with silt over the years and the tidal pools re-established, the wildlife returns. Families of black ducks and green head mallards take up residence again in these placid, salt-marsh ponds.

Given half a chance, Nature prevails.

Before the Ditching of the Marshes
Tom Reed, Waterman (NPS: 1971)

When duck eggs stop hatchin', there's something' wrong somewhere. And all our fiddler crabs died about ten years ago and the red mussels died in the marshes....I think the first thing they ought to do is plug every drainin' ditch in the whole world. And that would let the water go into the earth where it's supposed to be. It ain't supposed to be every time it hits the ground, run off in the river, run off in the ocean, washin' the dirt and filth and the pesticides in the river...and pollutin' the whole thing. This skeeter control ditched the whole place. They shouldn't oughta done it...what little (mosquito) spray got on the ground, its rushed right in these little drainage ditches, forced right out in our seafood bays, our seafood groves, and dat helps damage the arsters. The arsters quit catchin' for some reason or another, lost their spawns—they're floatin' around on top of the water, affectin' the fish, ya know, always scum or something' on top'll kill them. And they've ruint the whole works around here as fer as arster catch is concerned.

The beauty of the marshes, lush-green in summer, unfolds into an array of color during the first cool days of September and October. The spartina becomes tinged with light-brown hues, mixing its dulling tones with patches of reddening glasswort, flowering sea lavender, and the final summer blooming of the marsh mallows, with their white and pink flowers as big as dessert plates. As the first frost makes its visit, the afternoon skies turn a rich, clear blue with a trace of mackerel clouds. It is the best of times to spend here. For the night prowler, there is a bare chance of seeing, usually on a dark night with the moon down, an enchanting display of light. Along the edges of the marshes and in the tidal pools, a luminescence may suddenly glow, and then pulse as if regulated by a playful hand on a dimmer switch. The responsible source is likely to be an uncountable number of tiny protozoans, *Noctiluca scintillans*, the "shining light-of-the-night."

The western edge of the marsh usually marks the end of so-called tidal wetlands, which the bay waters may cover at the top of the tide. However, on higher ground, non-tidal wetlands are also frequently present, especially in poorly draining fields and woodlands. Non-tidal wetlands, like the tidal marshes, serve similar purposes of filtering groundwater runoff and providing wildlife habitat. Although non-tidal wetlands are more easily identified when boggy swamps are present, the types of vegetation are also an important indicator, even in the absence of surface water. American holly, highbush huckleberry, pepper bush, and a variety of low-lying ferns and mosses are sure signs of the typically hydrated soils. The wetlands may also alternate with "uplands," detectable by the appearance of laurel and tall bracken in the forest understory and more arable soils in the farmlands.

The pleasure of a walk through the forests of pine and mixed hardwoods is improved by wearing good boots and tough, long pants. April and May are good months for such hiking, after the dullness of winter and before the insects become a nuisance. Bright green shoots of skunk cabbage signal the warming weather. Nearby, usually in early May, a delicate companion is found among patches of pine and swamp oak. This is the pink lady-slipper, or moccasin flower, the regal orchid of these woodlands, with delicate blooms in the shape of tiny purses rising above the rotting loam of leaves and pine needles. The dank, lusty smell of the woods follows us everywhere along well-padded deer paths. A tall bull pine, the progenitor of a forest of tiny seedlings, towers over all, its smooth platelets of bark attesting to advanced maturity.

The lucky hiker may come across a Delmarva bay, an uncommon oddity found on the Lower Eastern Shore. It may suddenly appear in a clearing in the forest; though more likely it will be isolated near the edge of a marsh or in the middle of a low-lying farm field. The signs are classic: a patch of woods, usually no more than an acre or so, and often less, is rimmed with hardwoods that might include swamp oak, wild cherry, sour and sweet gum, tulip poplar, and sassafras. Entering through the wooded buffer, the explorer comes to a round, shallow pond, a natural depression in the silt-formed land. The fresh surface water may be knee-deep or more in the wet months, then nearly drying up in summer. Persimmon trees encircling the pond are a telling identification. The tree roots lie half in and half out of the water. Slim, twisted trunks and oddly curved branches weave an artistic design that could as well be found in a carefully pruned Japanese tea garden.

This is a herpetologist's paradise—a haven for endangered species of frogs and lizards. Raccoons prowl the water's edge for frogs. Opossums dine on the fruit of the persimmon tree, and then may hang from a limb by their tails to rest with a full belly. An isolated ecosystem is at work.

Another upland trail might follow along a small creek or narrow, free-flowing drain. As these salty rivulets turn brackish and mingle with the fresh flush of ground water and the oozings from underground springs, the hiker may come upon a sea fen. Fresh and salt water are at a stand-off and the stasis produces a cross between the course marsh grasses and a soft, mossier cushion. Here is another special ecosystem within the macro universe, filled with botanic and zoologic treasures. Embellishing this frame, exquisitely delicate woodland orchids lie in the moist soils nearby, barely detectable among the fallen pine needles and the rotting leaves of wetland-loving hardwoods.

Not all of the native flowers are as exotic as the woods orchids; other trails along ditchbanks and untended patches of open space yield the common yellow lily, yarrow and Queen Anne's lace. Even the lowly thistle and goldenrod—noxious to some people—have a valuable food-role in the wild community.

Farther inland lies the region's breadbasket—the soils that shaped an agro-economy that began with the early settlers. For the most part, several feet of arable soil rest on top of a layer of mushy clay. This stratum of clay is often the cause of poor drainage that is a bane to land developers, but it is also a cause of water-soaked land that is not all bad for the farmer. And beneath the clay is sandy, gravely sediment inherited from Pennsylvania and New Jersey thousands of years ago, forced southward by the plows of melting glaciers. The soil profiles are more complicated than this, yet it all adds up to farmlands that, on the average, are richer than that in neighboring Somerset and Wicomico Counties.

Studies of the relationship between the quality of the soil and the development of farming practices throughout the Lower Eastern Shore pose certain paradoxes. For example, why, in the colonial coastal watershed, was the growing of tobacco, which thrives on richer soils, abandoned more quickly than elsewhere on the Easter Shore? Perhaps due to the coincidence of falling tobacco prices, British blockades of coastal ports, and the persistent sentiment of doing things differently—of self-sufficiency—on the seaside. The seasiders turned to crops and crafts and trades that could either feed or sustain their local communities. They didn't want to depend on the outside world.

Living off the Land
Annie Hudson (THM: 2001)

Well, the day we were married we ate dinner at my mother's and then we were going to get married. As we went out, we saw my mother back of a pear tree in the orchard, and we wondered why she was there. After we were married, the next day or two, she said that she hid behind the tree to keep from seeing me going off to get married. So we went on to Ocean City and my husband had a room rented for the night. We went to get this room and they had rented it to somebody else. So then we had to come back to his folks, and in the middle of the night the cows got out and serenaded us. Yeah, I'll always remember that.

Well, when we got married we bought a farm and we had to work very hard. I worked out in the fields with my husband and then of a night I'd go up and we'd do our canning. We had our own meat (hogs), and we canned the meat and the sausage in a pressure cooker…and then it would be so late sometimes I would have to wash and hang the clothes out on the line by a lantern. Sometimes we'd be working in the fields, so tired and hungry that I would say, "I'm going up to the house, kill this chicken and

> dress it and fry it and have it for dinner." Hard work, yes. We also grew tomatoes; picked tomatoes every day. I picked tomatoes in every position, even laying down, picking tomatoes. And one day I had a sunstroke, picking those tomatoes. They had to take me up and lay me down on the porch. I never could bear to be out in the sun much after that.

Turning eastward from the Sinepuxent and Chincoteague Bays toward Assateague Island, a disembarking visitor finds one of the most accessible undeveloped seashores on the Atlantic coast. Despite human attempts over the past three centuries to domesticate this world-class beach, the island's natural state has generally prevailed. Along North Beach, the seven-mile stretch between the Ocean City Inlet and the Verrazano Bridge, the vegetation and variety of wildlife have been relatively subdued by the low elevation of the beach and frequent wash-overs from the sea. However, this barren sweep of beach has a certain beauty of its own. All is exposed to view: scurrying ghost crabs, a rare sea turtle on its way to bury eggs in the warm sand, the endangered piping plover, restless flights of the tiny sandpipers, and scattered families of Assateague wild horses.

On occasion, after a storm tide, the ribbed carcass of an old shipwreck rises for a time through the sand, only to be covered up again by the next storm. North Beach is truly one of the "sacred places" along the coastal bays. The serenity is unbroken by private vehicular traffic, which is prohibited. Only the cries of sea gulls and the roll of waves in the surf accompany the wandering beachcomber.

One anomaly on the island's north end is the high, vegetated knoll just below Ocean City Inlet, which was formed by deposits of dredged sand. The knoll has withstood several generations of high winds and tides and has supported the development of dense shrub that shelters a variety of wildlife. Sika, deer, and raccoons hunker down during the day, avoiding the beachcombers and bathers. A family of red foxes has built its den among the bayberry roots and, on occasion, used the cavities among the jetty rocks as whelping boxes.

Hiking down the beach towards the Verrazano Bridge, the bayberry grows taller and begins to merge with scrub pines. Groundsel joins to form a salt-resistant bushy barrier between marsh and emerging woodland—these shrubby trees so gnarled and tangled that old-timers disparagingly called them "kinks" bushes. Still farther south, beyond the range of this particular hike, low-lying forest and still thicker brush stand out behind a protective dune line. Below the Virginia line in the Chincoteague National Wildlife Refuge, the loblolly pines now mature to nearly full size—75-80 feet or more in height—and mix with pin and red oaks. Sandy woodland paths covered with pine needles lead off into the brush. Wavy tentacles of poison ivy reach out from the thickets—a caution sign for hikers, yet one of the food staples for the horses and deer.

Naturalists classify these "eco-zones" into at least three main communities—diverse, yet interdependent. Starting on the ocean side of the island and working westward from the surf toward the bay, the first natural community comprises the protective primary dune line, supported by beach grasses anchoring the wind-driven sand. Moving westward behind the protective dunes, a transitional zone of low thickets leads into the more secure woodland community. These forested areas harbor much of the wildlife on the island. Their wooded shelter and soils enriched by organic matter also provided a means of livelihood for the colonial settlers. Later, the natural beauty attracted various schemes for real estate development, all of which proved ill-fated. The third island community is the marsh, which, like the marshes fringing the mainland, is ecologically important as a breeding ground and nursery for marine life. Historically, these marshy aprons on each side of the bays have migrated westward, sometimes in tandem, as part of a rhythmic rollover in the face of rising sea levels. However, this natural drift has been affected by man-made "dune lines" on the island and shoreline construction on the mainland, which may resist for a time the push of rising waters.

So, where can the Assateague wild horses get a decent drink of fresh water? Water, of course, is available in the isolated ponds, like oases in the desert. Here, rainwater and shallow groundwater springs collect in small sinkholes, much like the Delmarva bays on the mainland. A diverse wildlife community comes to drink—horses, deer, foxes, raccoons, rabbits, and, in the Chincoteague National Wildlife Refuge, the endangered species of Delmarva Peninsula fox squirrels. All presumably benefit from the "sweet" water devoid of fertilizers, pesticides, and other land-borne chemicals. However, the wild horses might survive in any case, since they have adjusted to the intake of saline fluid foraged from the marsh plants.

A good time to observe and listen to life at the ponds is just before nightfall, such as on a mild evening in early autumn, when the sound of tree frogs, crickets, and chuck-will's-widows explode at dusk to blend with the steady mumble of the surf. The quiet watcher may see the elusive black duck begin to pitch, coming in singles and pairs, until the pond surface is nearly covered with dark silhouettes. Then one hears a "high-ball" call far out into the night, which is answered in turn nearby. Soon comes a whistle of wings and a fluttering dark shape against the moon drops in to join the crowd. The chuckling feed-calls that combine in the darkening night, punctuated by the bugle-like call of a sika, can send a shiver down the spine.

This biodiversity of wildlife is displayed on a transect across the island from surf side to bay side. Trails have been laid out by the National Park Service to cover these major eco-zones, and guided tours are conducted daily in season. Casual hikers explore on their own.

Visitors to Assateague Island are, at first sight, fascinated by the wild ponies, whose fame and equine status have been secured by Marguerite Henry's popular children's book, *Misty of Chincoteague*. The "pony" misnomer, however appealing it sounds to the youngster, may be on the way out. The National Park Service is intent on correcting the genetic record. A horse is a horse.

According to popular legend, the horses came from a shipwrecked Spanish vessel—possibly the *San Lorenzo* that reportedly ran aground off Assateague in 1820 with ninety-five small horses on board. If the horses made it to shore, it is likely that the animals were added to the existing stock that were grazed on the island by early settlers. Though now classified as a "desirable exotic species," the horses have become a problematic attraction due to their increased numbers and their impact on the island's ecology through over-grazing. Visitors are also cautioned against feeding the horses; they bite. As well, beware when the mares are in heat, and the stallions begin to snort and paw the ground when approached.

Research was initiated in 1986 to develop a contraceptive program for controlling the horse population, which in 1965 was counted at 21 on the Maryland portion of the island and had grown to 167 by 1984. After considerable experimentation by program-developer Jay Kirkpatrick, an innovative method was adopted comprising dart-delivered injectable steroids. A further refinement in the contraceptive program has led to the use of a vaccine that causes an immunologic response rendering the horses temporarily infertile.

Assateague Wild Horses
Jay Kirkpatrick (NPS: 2004)

My most poignant moment, and I even remember it was March of 1991, was when I found the carcass of M-4, and she had died a natural death—she was an old mare—up on the north end. And it wasn't until that moment that I fully understood that what we were doing (birth control) had allowed her to live her entire life on this island without threat of removal, without disruption of her family group, family harem, or anything like that....It allowed her the dignity of dying where she was born, having a life on Assateague without interruption. The only harassment were my darts once a year. It was at that moment...I understood what this could do for horses.

There's a dozen other super-memorable moments. One of them occurred two thousand miles from here, and that was after that spring of 1988 when I got those twenty-six mares darted. We came out in the fall and collected the urine samples and I took them back to my laboratory in Billings, Montana. And I did the hormone essay with those samples that would tell us who was pregnant and who wasn't. The results were done on about four o'clock on a Friday afternoon and there was not another living human being in the science building. The secretaries had gone home. There wasn't even a custodian to go hug. I watched this tape roll off a machine called liquid scintillation counter: twenty-six groups of numbers. I didn't even have to do the calculations. You learn to just look at the raw numbers and you can tell whether the horse is pregnant or not. We had six control numbers and three came off pregnant and three came off non-pregnant, and then, one by one, twenty-six mares that we had treated—non-pregnant, non-pregnant, non-pregnant, non-pregnant, and there was not a single soul to tell, to hug, to kiss, to shout to. No one in that building, and I stood there in front of that machine with this tape and that was my life. I mean, this is what I had spent sixteen years trying to achieve and there it was in my hand, this piece of tape, and no one in the building.

Less famous and much shyer than horses are the sika. Though commonly referred to as a deer, the sika is actually a small member of the elk family, of Asian origin, introduced to the island in the 1920s. According to the late Turner Cropper, a Boy Scout at the time and later a fine waterman, the local troop purchased "several" sika near Philadelphia and brought them to Ocean City for the summer—charging tourists parading along the boardwalk a few pennies per viewing. The revenues helped finance a trip to New York for the Boy Scouts at the end of the vacation season.

The sika were rewarded by being turned loose on North Beach and have thrived ever since. Another stocking of sika on Assateague Island is reported to have come at about the same time from a herd that had been established earlier on Taylor's Island in the Chesapeake Bay. Whatever their initial source, sika have acclimatized well to Assateague Island, sharing habitat with the larger, native white-tailed deer.

Selected examples of the fish and bird life of the bays tell much about the current condition of this ecosystem. One of the most contested species is the blue crab, currently the subject of heated debate as to population levels and sustainable commercial harvests. Scientific interest is also focused on the lethal effect on crabs in the coastal bays by

Hematodinium. This algal-like, pathogenic organism appears to be related to *Pfisteria*, which has received much greater attention for being involved in extensive fish kills in tributaries of the Chesapeake Bay and other Mid-Atlantic estuaries. Further study of *Hematodinium* may also reveal important links between the pathogenic state of this organism and factors that impact water quality and harvest levels in the coastal bays.

> ## Crabs, Once Upon a Time
> ## Clarence Pilchard, Girdletree (TP: 2004)
>
> **I remember one day Dad came in off the bay (c. 1953) and we had eighteen barrels of crabs—big crabs—that's maybe four bushels in every barrel. At that time, the market had so many crabs the man would only pay us two dollars a barrel; that works out to about fifty cents a bushel. Why, a bushel of bait was five dollars—herring. Dad said, "I'll not sell them for that," so we dumped them over the side. The market wasn't always like that….Most of the time, the men made their money during the peeler crab season (the peelers to be shed into soft crabs). And the buyers would be waiting for you at the dock. They would start out offering at 25 cents, then 26, 27. And you might have 15-20,000 peelers. Now that was a lot of money in the fifties.**

For the crabber, the most productive spots in the bays are usually found in several feet or more of quiet water, a good distance from Ocean City Inlet; the farther from strong tidal currents, the better. Early morning and late afternoon, preferably on the rising tide, are favored crabbing times. One of the better crabbing stations accessible by land is the dock at the state boat ramp by the entrance to the Verrazano Bridge. However, recreational crabbing, once highly productive throughout the coastal bays, has waned due to increasing competition from commercial crab pots that fill the bays in season.

Still, recreational opportunities remain for young and old to poke along the edges of the shorelines with a crab net—search for prizes of soft crabs hiding from predators in the beds of bay grasses. On the right moon and tide, a disturbed "softie" will surely rise slowly from under a bed of sea lettuce; and what youngster will not have been transformed forever by scooping the crab into the net and then holding that soft, wrinkled creature in the palm of a hand, utterly intrigued by this magic of shellfish growth.

The flounder is the prized finfish for most anglers, although sea trout (weak fish), striped bass (rockfish), and croakers (hardheads) run right behind in popularity. One of the fisherman's grandest times is to anchor up in a nice hole along the marsh bank, anytime from August to October, when the tide is coming full in the late afternoon and early evening. The fisherman lets out a nice piece of ripe peeler crab or a small live spot into the current and waits quietly for that barely perceptible tap-tap from a huge "tide-runner" with the yellow belly. The next pull comes with a whoosh, and the result may be the biggest sea trout the fishermen will ever catch, up to almost a yard long and fat from feeding on marsh-clinging life in the food chain.

What many fishermen don't realize is that after the more common grey trout has left for warmer water, its more colorful and tastier cousin, the speckled trout, has now moved in to provide the knowing angler with excellent sport until the end of fall. Schools of "speckles" will feed along unlikely drop-offs between sandy shoals and deeper water; and at daybreak and sunset on the right tide, as flights of migrating waterfowl move across a crisp sky, these moments on the coastal bays are all too brief.

The confirmed rock fisherman may similarly reminisce about fishing the Ocean City Inlet on a cold, late fall evening. The red drum fisherman thinks of the surf on Assateague in the spring, when the dogwood trees begin to bloom, and in the early autumn as the first maple leaf turns to gold.

But not all the sought-after fish grow into whoppers. The small, slender silversides, or "shiners," are among the several species of minnows that are purchased or netted for bait to catch the larger fish, especially flounder. But what many fishermen don't realize is that the lowly shiners they may discard at the end of the day are the prized "white bait" served in the best European restaurants.

> ## Living off the Bay
> ## Miles Hancock, Chincoteague (NPS: 1971)
>
> I made a living out of that (fishing and clamming) until de eel grass left. Now, I didn't know that de eel grass was my livin', see. I used to curse it in de summertime. I had a shanty and it had a cove…my houseboat laid right along here. But in the summer, take the wind dissa way, it would float this here grass back in here and overnight that would gas…and gas is there everyday a while. We used to curse it because we didn't like there isn't any way we could clam. But that was our livin' then (the eel grass). We didn't know it. Eels would stay with us during the winter, and up there in the channel I've seen forty to fifty head up there a giggin' 'em like this, with a eel speer. Makin' ten, fifteen, twenty dollars a day. I used to think with my fikes and pounds (nets) that if there weren't no eel grass I would make a killin' 'cause they'd have to run faster. I used to make seven or eight hundred dollars a spring–short season. But the first year the eel grass left, 'bout three hundred dollars…and the next year I made about thirty-five dollars. Well I turned it over into something' to pay me, see.

Much like oysters and other mollusks, the hard-shell clams, or quahogs, are water-filterers and perform as ecological vacuum cleaners. Healthy populations are vital to good water quality, and fortunately the clam is in better shape in the bays than most other underwater species. It's an incredible reproducer. For the recreational clammer, the most productive clam beds may be found along the sandy shoals behind Assateague Island and north of the Rt. 50 Bridge in the Isle of Wight Bay. Buying or renting a clam rake is a low-cost investment in a day of fun and food-gathering. However, as with other important fisheries, the increased commercial harvest pressure has resulted in conflict between the commercial clammer and recreational and environmental groups. A particular concern is the scarifying of the bottom of the bays by the hydraulic clam dredges, which may be impacting any number of other benthic, bay-bottom resources.

The diamondback terrapin is a somewhat neglected member of the coastal bays, even though it is a Maryland state symbol, the name of the University of Maryland athletic teams, and richly connected to the social and culinary history of Delmarva. The name "terrapin" is of Algonquian origin, and the local Indians feasted on it. The epicurean status of the terrapin has fluctuated over the ages, due in part to the available numbers at the time and the culinary tastes of the day.

When plentiful, the terrapin was fed to servants *ad nauseam*. Maryland law once proscribed its too-frequent feeding to slaves. Later, in times of scarcity, terrapin soup became a prized dish of the upper crust and found its way on the best tables of Baltimore, Philadelphia, and New York. This was a classic at the old Hotel Rennert in Baltimore and other grand old eating establishments that have long since perished. Now it has all but disappeared from menus throughout the land.

Today, the terrapin is more important as an indicator of the bays' health, the proverbial canary in the coal mine. That their numbers are believed to be in decline in some areas of the bays may be due to two principal factors: the profusion of crab pots that can entrap and drown the terrapin, and the loss of natural shorelines (to bulkheads and riprap) that normally would allow the female terrapin to crawl onto the sandy shore to lay her eggs. Efforts to help sustain terrapin populations in Maryland's tidewater regions have been spearheaded in the coastal bays by the Assateague Coastal Trust, through the distribution of terrapin-excluding devices (installed in the openings of crab pots) and wire cages that may be placed over terrapin nests to protect the eggs from predation by raccoons, black snakes, crows, gulls, and wandering cats and dogs.

Another portent of the bays' condition is the horseshoe crab, one of the planet's oldest creatures, which is presently in decline after having survived for more than 300 million years.

The shrinkage of suitable shoreline habitat for crab spawning may be part of the problem. Intensive harvesting is probably a more significant factor. There just aren't enough of these primitive crustaceans to go around. Commercial watermen find a good market for the crabs, selling them as bait for eel pots and whelk traps. Scientists want the crabs to extract their blood for processing into biological agents to be used in diagnosing spinal meningitis and other diseases. A substance in the crab's shell is also used to promote healing around surgical sutures, and the crab's eyes have revealed much about how the human eye works.

A good time to observe horseshoe crabs is in late spring, during their spawning season, when migrating shore birds, especially the red knots, are filling up on crabs' eggs to sustain them on their journeys to nesting sites farther north. And that should be reason enough to protect this venerable crab.

The decline of traditional commercial catches and the tightening of fisheries regulations keep watermen on the move to find other species to harvest profitably. Witness the increase in trapping whelks from the ocean floor and in the potting of eels in the coastal bays to supply a lucrative overseas market. A familiar cycle is repeating itself: abundance followed by unsustainable fishing pressures.

Bird life is likewise a story of historic abundance and then a diminishing over time from the impacts of development and increased pressure from hunters and fishermen. However, the picture here is somewhat brighter. Efforts to preserve sustainable populations are paying off for some feathered species. Once a victim of the widespread use of the pesticide DDT, the osprey has made a dramatic comeback along the coastal bays, as elsewhere. It is common once again to see the osprey returning across the bay from its hunt, a menhaden or bluefish clutched tightly in its talons to be delivered to a nest of open mouths poking from a nest atop one of the channel markers.

In its exacting, late-winter return to the nesting site, the osprey may also prove to be an early harbinger of climate change; any deviation from its finely-set timer could sound an ominous alarm.

The number of bald eagles is up as well. Two pairs are nesting on Assateague Island as of this writing. Another breeding pair has taken up residence at Rum Pointe Golf Course, and an increasing number of pairs are seen along Trappe Creek and the forested mainland of the Chincoteague Bay. The sighting of eagles out fishing or prowling along the beach for a meal of wild duck has become routine.

Another upbeat story concerns the peregrine falcon, which, like the osprey, was nearly decimated by DDT. Watching these marvelous hunting machines patrolling the beach during their migratory stopover in September and October is one of the high points of the birder's season. Though the falconer may no longer take birds from the island for use in falconry, this is still an important location for banding peregrines for scientific study.

Above all, it may be the great variety of the smaller shorebirds that delight bird watchers along the coastal bays. The peninsular geography of the watershed, generous habitats, and temperate climate attract both nesting and wintering birds in season, plus the migratory stopovers. It's a year-long event and, at times, the sighting of shorebirds, waders, and waterfowl is unsurpassed on the Atlantic Coast. Yet this is another case of near-tragedy. Once-abundant shorebirds, such as the Eskimo curlew and golden plover, were following the passenger pigeon into extinction. Technologic improvements in firearms added to the slaughter. Hunters gunned down unwary flocks by the boatload and wagon-load, often with abandon, to see how many could be killed in a day. Waterfowl were similarly affected by the practice of "market gunning."

Fortunately, waterbird populations began to stabilize, and later to improve for some species after enactment in 1918 of the Federal Migratory Game Act. This regulation prohibited the shooting of shorebirds, and eventually the shooting of all species of wildfowl and game for the commercial market—a milestone conservation measure. However, in the time following the initial enactment to add species to the list of prohibited targets, many shorebirds in already endangered numbers were whittled down to a size that minimized their opportunity for full recovery.

The piping plover, though still on the endangered species list, is making some progress on the extreme north and south ends of the island. The novice birder may mistake the piping plover for the semipalmated plover, or even the black bellied plover in transition to winter plumage. But that only adds to the challenge and enjoyment of birdwatching.

When the birding and wild horse-watching have run their course, it may be time for the enterprising adventurer to begin foraging for lunch or dinner. Underwater, underfoot, and within arm's reach throughout the coastal bays is a bountiful variety of edible plants—the same that supplemented a diet of fish and game that nourished the Assateague Indians for centuries and fed many of the later settlers during lean times. That so many of the first colonists in Virginia, surrounded by a similar abundance of natural foods, reportedly starved to death is astounding.

Nutritious ingredients in the wild are still here—for identification, if not always for the plucking, by skilled foragers. Strict rules govern the harvesting of vegetation on the island, and property owners on the mainland are wary of uninvited visitors collecting supper in their front yards. Yet with a bit of scouting and botanical study, a feast can be prepared of fresh salads in the form of wild lettuce, sea blite, orach, purslane, sour sorrel, and lovage, among many other equally tasty plants. Seasonings are to be had from poor man's pepper, and seawater is the best medium for steaming crabs. Desserts of beach plums, fox grapes, crab apples, and persimmons are easy as pie.

However, it is not recommended that the amateur attempt to make marshmallows from the namesake plant found commonly along the marsh, though this non-native species was once a source for confecting the campfire favorite. In fact, the mallow has been better known throughout history as an elixir for symptomatic treatment of respiratory ailments, such as bronchitis, persistent coughing, and sore throats. As far back as early Roman days, Pliny the Elder, an observant naturalist in his time, wrote, "Whosoever shall take a spoonful of the Mallows, shall that day be free of all diseases that may come to him."

Glasswort is yet another of the common, and most recognizable, edibles to be found in the marsh. Its salty, crunchy flavor is a substitute for bits of bacon in a mixed salad of wild greens, or it is fine by itself, accompanied by a simple vinaigrette sauce.

Virtually all of these wild foods are more nutritious than their supermarket counterparts. Nature's organic ingredients abound with vitamins, minerals, and all the trace elements. However, the seabeach amaranth—the piping plover of green plants—is to be avoided. Though related to the common varieties of edible amaranth "greens" found on the mainland, the seabeach variety is endangered. Its comeback on the island is being assisted by careful replanting and enclosing with wire protective devices.

Wild appetizers and meatier main-course possibilities can round out an impressive "tasting" menu: fish fresh-caught from either the surf or bay; clams raked from the bay shallows, served raw or steamed; crabs cooked in the briny seawater; and, to wrap up, a confection of wild fruit for dessert. This can become a lifetime pursuit. The identification and preparation of these and many other wild foods along the seaside have been well covered in Euell Gibbons' *Stalking the Blue-Eyed Scallop* and other worthy books in his *Stalking* series, as well as in other, more current, publications.

Bounty of the Bay
Don Bowden, "Teaguer" (NPS: 1978)

The main food was fried oysters or oyster stew, almost exclusive. I mean, if you had oysters, very, very few people had crab sandwich or a soft crab sandwich in a restaurant. They had fish but very little. But every restaurant that ever opened there (around Chincoteague) you couldn't make it without fried oysters and oyster stew, because then they had plenty of oysters, and oysters were big and fat...and Chincoteague oysters were famous at that time. They were shipped all over the world, just about, or all over the Eastern part of the United States. In barrels, shipped 'em in

barrels, with a burlap top and a lid, a wooden hook on the top, and top nailed so the oysters wouldn't fall out if they turned the barrel over.

Yeah, and steamers? They used to sell oyster steam. Fill a wire basket that would hold about two quarts of oysters in the shell, and you'd have a boiler on that's about two feet long and about a foot wide and with boiling water. You turn that on about six in the evening 'cause people like to eat steamed oysters at night, usually. And they would come in and get a steamer, and you'd put this wire basket in this boiling water for about three minutes. Then when you took it out, all the oysters were open and then you take it into the counter and the guy would have a saucer.

If one can no longer scavenge enough wild oysters for dinner along the marsh banks or in the shallows by the islands, there's still the opportunity to search out the old oyster-packing cans from a once-thriving industry, which have found a home in local antique shops. What used to be thrown away like empty pet food cans can now bring a few hundred dollars, or even more for the rare coastal bays variety. Savor the memory and the collector's pleasure, if not the fresh oyster.

Assateague Wild Horses

Pony-sized, the wild horses roam free on the island and have become perhaps the most famous single attraction. Despite careful management of the herd's population, their numbers and grazing habits threaten the island's ecosystem.

Photo courtesy of Mike Gatty

Sika: Shy, Quiet Residents of Assateague Island

Sika family on the move…and close up. Virtually unheralded, this miniature member of the elk family is gaining in numbers and growing in popularity with visitors to the island. Spending much of the day hugging the edges of thickets, sika become quite visible and less shy in the early morning and at dusk.

Photos by Mike Gatty

Dressed for Fishing, 1920s Style

Fishing prior to the '33 hurricane differed from the sport of today. There were neither harbors nor marinas in Ocean City, and private fishing boats were few. Seasonal visitors depended on guides for boat trips or to lead them to surf fishing spots by hiking, on horseback, or in beach buggies. Judging by the footwear, this had been a boat-fishing trip. Sweaters and jackets suggest a time just after the heat of summer. The fine catch of sea trout would have been typical in September.

.Photo by Melville Quillen (c. 1920): collection of the author

Imperiled Shore Birds

Market shooting and recreational hunting of shore birds in the early 20th century threatened extinction of many once-numerous shoreline waders. The federal ban imposed in 1918 on shore bird hunting spared most, but not all, species.

Photo courtesy of Taylor House Museum

Waiting for Dinner

Ospreys in historic numbers are returning again on schedule in late March to stake claims to their territorial nests atop channel markers in the coastal bays.

Photo by Mike Gatty

Marsh and Mainland

The marshmallow, in the white and pink of late-summer bloom, color the marsh just beyond normal high tide. In addition to its hibiscus-family appearance, the mallow may be the most versatile of the marsh plants: once a base-ingredient for its namesake confection; a nourishing food plant; a soothing brew for treating symptoms of cough and cold; and poultice for applying to wounds.

The Delmarva bay is a zoological oasis and a good starting point on the annual Great Worcester Herp Search. Among the reptiles and amphibians that might be found here are red-backed salamanders, Fowler's toads, box turtles, rat snakes, chorus-frog tadpoles, and leopard and green frogs. Rooted in the shallow, fresh water, wavy persimmon trees become heavy with fruit in the fall and attract yet another set of wild foragers.

Photos by Mike Gatty (top) and the author (bottom)

IV

Skins worn proudly by the Indian chief
could not assuage his final grief;
but now the deer that gather at dusk
take the revenge the chief could not,
fattening on corn from the farmer's lot.

Assateague Indians and English Settlers: A Nearly Vanished Legacy

A flinty shard barely appears through the sediment, which, during a coastal storm not long ago, had eroded from the clay bank and accumulated in clumps at the high-tide line on the mainland edge of the Sinepuxent Bay. The arrowhead is beautifully crafted from ochre-colored stone. A careful examination reveals that the projectile is over 5,000 years old. The chiseled stone is not indigenous.

When, and from where, did these Native Americans come? Are any of the local Indians still surviving? This is part of the mystery of a sadly abused tribe that left its archeological mark, yet has nearly vanished as a full-blooded race.

52

Look for the signs of Assateague Indian heritage along Maryland's coastal bays, and, aside from place names, they appear at first to be absent. Few descendants of this isolated tribe have survived here, or elsewhere, to tell their story. There are neither museums nor permanent exhibits in the immediate area dedicated to these first inhabitants of the seaside. No dwellings are left standing to confirm the accounts of the first European explorers to touch these shores. A microcosm of civilization that lasted nearly 10,000 years quickly came to an end, as if removed by the direct impact of a severe hurricane. In this case, the storm was the relentless surge of English settlers, accompanied by a definitive massacre and the white man's diseases.

On peering more closely, the faint imprints of an earlier civilization may be observed along the coastal bays. On a spring day, a walk over freshly-plowed fields often yields a few finely-honed arrowheads. Wading at low tide along the shallow edges of the shoreline can turn up the bits and pieces of primitive pottery, stone utensils, and a surprising variety of projectile points used for hunting game and fowl and for spearing fish. Piles of long-discarded oyster and clam shells—Indian middens—can still be found in a few undisturbed woods near the water. Refuse pits are occasionally uncovered in the course of land development. Burial areas are still being discovered, as well. These relics have identified the Assateague Indians as accomplished hunters, fishermen, and roving food-gatherers. It was a way of life to be copied, but never fully matched, among later settlers.

Gene Parker (TP: 2004)

I don't know exactly how I got caught up in hunting for artifacts, but it probably all goes back to playing Cowboys-and-Indians when I was a young kid, maybe five years old. Then going to the Saturday matinee movies and seeing the shoot-'em-ups. And later the idea of finding arrowheads and all these other relics right here, right under our noses, all over the place. Now that was exciting, oh boy! I guess it was really the

excitement of the hunt. Then I was growing up and I had this principal at Selbyville School and he was really into it, going out on these digs every weekend, mostly over in the Gumboro swamp. He had a huge—I mean huge—collection.

It's amazin' what you can still find if you know where to look and what you're lookin' for. A piece of high ground in a field when it's just been plowed in the spring. Lots of places along the bays, I'm not going to tell you exactly where. My most interestin' finds? Maybe the pieces of this one old Indian pot. I just saw a piece showing there in the mud along the marsh down towards Girdletree, and the more I scraped around the more pieces I found. The fun part has been trying to put the pieces back together. It's like a jig-saw puzzle, each piece has got to fit perfectly. If it's even a little off, it's not the right piece. Then I got this axe head here—it's my favorite—that I found along Manklin Creek. This beautiful black piece of stone polished down to perfection, lying there I don't know how long just picking up barnacles. An archeologist who looked at it said maybe 10,000 years old. I want to take it somewhere and have it dated, maybe the Smithsonian. Well, I try not to take anything that's politically incorrect, although I know that there are people who object to what I do. But I can't help thinking that putting this axe head and some of the other pieces I've collected in a local museum, which I have been doing all along, will interest some school kid into learnin' more about the history behind all this here. I hope so.

Actually, it was your dad who got me goin' on this other stuff—treasure huntin'. That was back in the 60s when he was goin' all over the ocean looking for old Spanish wrecks, getting himself thrown in Castro's jail, and doin' all kinds of things that sounded like real adventure to me. And when he gave me this old Spanish silver coin, or maybe it was another one like it, that's all it took to set me off. I spent a lot of money chasing down pots of gold that usually weren't where we thought they might be. But it's all been worth it. I'd do it all over again.

At one time it was generally believed that the Assateague Indians settled locally sometime early in the Christian era. However, this notion, along with many other long-held beliefs about the Assateague Indians, has been discredited by more recent information. What is now fairly certain is that wandering bands of Indians, probably sub-tribes of the Algonquian Nation, were present on the seaside and elsewhere on Delmarva as early as 10,000 B.C.—centuries prior to records of advancing civilizations in the Middle East or in South and Central America. One theory has been that the first local bands came from the nomadic peoples of Asia who crossed the frozen, humped-up connection between Siberia and Alaska near the end of the last major Ice Age. If true—and this theory is under challenge—this migration probably occurred before the rise of sea levels would leave behind only the barest exposure of island atolls in the North Pacific and Arctic Seas.

However, even these dates of Indian origins may be conservative, as anthropologists have now cited the possibility of human presence in the Mid-Atlantic region some 19,000 years ago, based on the discovery of a single spearhead in Western Maryland. If so, how and from where did humans get here at that time? The answers to such questions are a wide-open field for study, as is much of the under-researched prehistoric period.

In any event, around 900 A.D., the Indian tribes of the Delmarva Peninsula—mostly sharing certain Algonquian characteristics and dialect—evolved from a primitive Stone Age culture to a more sedentary and advancing life-style, marked by the planting of crops and greater sophistication of craft work. The Assateagues are generally believed to have been one of four major tribes on Maryland's Eastern Shore, along with the Pocomokes, their closest neighbors, and the Nanticokes and Choptanks, who made their camps by the rivers that carry their names today. Historical references are also made to local Indians called Kickotanks (or Kegotanks) and Gingoteagues, though these probably comprised sub-tribes of the Assateagues in the coastal bays watershed. Typical of recorded history in Maryland, much more is known about life along the Chesapeake Bay, and so it is that details about the Assateagues are but a short, though fascinating, chapter.

The earliest reports about the Assateague Indians came from European explorers who described them as speaking a different dialect, of lighter skin, slight in stature, and less hostile than Indians encountered in the Chesapeake Bay watershed by Captain John Smith and other early colonizers. The Assateagues were uncommonly friendly. This has raised the question about whether the coastal Indians were an entirely different breed, much as outsiders would say about seaside inhabitants for centuries to come. It could be that geographic isolation just made them that way.

Protected by the interior geography of swamp and tangled forests, the Assateague Indians appeared to show little concern for attacks from hostile tribes. It was an attitude that carried over into the colonial era, as the English settlers tended to ignore the lawmakers and power-brokers of Baltimore and Annapolis. Unlike the Indian towns of the Nanticokes and the Choptanks, which were enclosed by heavy-timbered palisades, the headquarters and seasonal camps of the Assateagues were wide open. The principal headquarters, or werewonce (also translated as "king"), was probably located near the headwaters of the St. Martin River behind Ocean City—though exact locations of early Indian sites, even if known, are unpublicized. Political correctness, though coming late, is now the rule in leaving untouched, and preserving these sites of Indian heritage.

Outpost camps were also set up seasonally to exploit the best hunting and fishing grounds, and more explicit evidence of these locations is available. One such site has been studied on the mainland near the Verrazano Bridge. The Rum Pointe Golf Course covers much of this former campground, and some features of archaeological significance have been preserved. Excavations of water holes on the golf course brought up stone relics dating back as far as 5,000-10,000 B.C. Storage pits were also identified in the preconstruction phase of the golf course, and these have been stabilized, though left unmarked in the rough near Green Creek. Indian shell middens are also to be found in small piles among the pines behind the back nine. Although the middens may be largely attributed to the feeding on oysters, clams, and mussels, the Assateagues also minted their currency, or wampum, from pretty shell fragments. Polished mussel shells, usually strung like beads, were referred to as roanoke, and the purple shard of the clam as peak.

Petrified peach pits were reportedly found in an Indian refuse pit on nearby Green Point, possibly contradicting the more traditional notion that English settlers brought the first peach trees to America. Undoubtedly, there are still such treasures to be discovered up and down the shorelines of the coastal bays, along with further insight into this poorly documented Indian tribe.

One curiosity gleaned from the spare historical accounts is that the Indian women had assumed a peer role. The tribal queen's status was equal, if not superior, to the king's in some respects. Her maternal line normally determined the succession of kings, or emperors, unlike the practice among monarchies in Europe. The queen also rated her own separate camp, which was reportedly located a few miles to the south of the king's headquarters, possibly at the head of one of the small tributaries feeding into Newport Bay near Berlin. How often the king and queen got together is a matter of conjecture. Apparently the Assateagues, like other Delmarva tribes, had liberal views about mating and marriage.

While the Assateague Indian males continued their traditions of fishing and hunting, the women carried out essential, heavy-duty tasks of planting and caring for the maize and other crops that were beginning to support a more stationary life. A similar social structure evolved during the later build-up of Ocean City: while the women ran the boarding houses and motels and restaurants to cater to a booming tourism industry, the men were often taken up with hunting and fishing.

The comparison of Indian dwellings to the homes of the early settlers is more of a stretch, although simplicity and functional forms may be similarly considered. Symmetrically designed Indian dwellings were framed with poles and sided with weavings of reeds, the gaps plugged with tree moss and the oval-domed exterior shingled with bark. Holes left open in the top-center served as a flue for the open fires, used for heating and cooking. Platform beds were covered with soft animal pelts.

In the early 1900s, the popular "4-square" house would seem to have borrowed from this primitive design. Simple, severely symmetrical, and functional, the layout featured a fireplace or furnace located dead-center in the floor plan. Many 4-square homes are still standing, though somewhat out of fashion. More recent owners have enclosed the porches, added wings, and modernized the interiors, but the basic framework is still there, as indelible as the Indian hut.

The Assateagues also established a pattern of transportation by canoe that endured well into the twentieth century, and is even now regaining popularity for paddling around in the more sheltered waters. However, unlike the featherweight craft of today, it is likely that the Assateagues' dugouts were often hollowed out of heavy, rot-resistant logs taken from bald cypress trees, or possibly from red cedars. One probable source of the logs was in the boggy lands at Shingle Landing Prong along the Assawoman Bay. Today, a stand of bald cypress still survives in the prong, one of the northernmost groves of cypress in the United States.

Inland trails were restricted within the narrow coastal watershed and ended a comfortable distance from the more aggressive Indian tribes along the headwaters of the Chesapeake Bay tributaries. One principal overland trail ran north-south along the low rise separating the coastal and Chesapeake Bay watersheds, stretching from near the Assateagues' headquarters to the domain of the Pocomoke Indians. The same Indian trail would be beaten down later by horses and wagons of the English settlers. Somewhat extended, it then became known as the Delaware Trail and connected the squabbling European-settled territories that would eventually achieve statehood as Maryland and Delaware. This same trail would also be renamed the Philadelphia Post Road, a pony express route of colonial times. The villages of Snow Hill and Berlin took life from the increasing commerce along this rutted, and sometimes impassable, road. Today, it is the heavily trafficked Route 113.

The first Europeans landed on these local shores only a little more than a generation after Columbus discovered America in 1492. This first chapter of recorded history, the so-called Contact Period, as Indian met European, began with Giovanni da Verrazano, an Italian explorer. Verrazano, sailing the ship *Dauphine* under charter of Francis I of France, is believed to have come ashore in 1524 somewhere near Ocean City. Verrazano did not find the sought-after shortcut to the spice riches of the Far East. But he did report finding a beautiful wooded "Arcadia" during his brief inspection of the Delmarva shoreline. As a souvenir, Verrazano took away a young Indian boy—a seemingly insensitive gesture in return for the friendly treatment accorded by the local Indians. In belated recognition of the Verrazano visit, the explorer's name was given to the bridge built in 1962 spanning the Sinepuxent Bay.

The Indians may have forgotten Verrazano by the time 35-year old Henry Norwood and his fellow English passengers, a party of sixteen men and three women, were abandoned by their ship's crew just over a century later on an icy, wind-raked, and foreboding beach somewhere near Fenwick. It was early January in 1650. The weather had turned bitter beyond present-day standards, for this was during the "Little Ice Age" when an extraordinary cycle of cold winters lasted for several hundred years. At the point of starvation, under-clothed, and freezing, and cannibalizing those members of the party who did perish, the remaining survivors were rescued at a point of total desperation by the Kickotank band of Assateague Indians. Despite a serious language barrier, the English were treated with unexpected hospitality and then nursed back to health, apparently dining well on wild turkeys, swans, geese, venison, and on various gruels made from hickory nuts and ground corn.

During their convalescence, a member of the Indian tribe traveled to the Eastern Shore of Virginia and returned with Jenkin Price, a white trapper, and his Indian side-kick, Jake. The two served as interpreters and arranged to guide Norwood's party to the newly established colony on the Eastern Shore of Virginia. Though the distance was probably no more than fifty miles, the journey by foot was arduous for the tender-footed and still-weakened survivors of this remarkable saga. Their story, nevertheless, had a happy ending. Surviving members of the party continued on to Williamsburg and other westward points. Norwood became a legend, lived to tell endlessly his tale of survival, and played a prominent and prosperous role in English politics.

Norwood's account of the rescue was preserved in his journal, *Voyage to Virginia–1649*, and recently recreated in an entertaining book by Sharon Himes called *Cavalier's Adventure*. Norwood's journal has told us most of what is known today about life among the Assateagues in the twilight of their Stone Age, just ten short years before the first wave of English settlers.

Shortly after Norwood's saga, the European immigration rapidly expanded northward from Accomack. Land grants were being made on large parcels along the coastal bays, beginning in the latter part of the 1600s. The "land rush" followed a campaign in 1659 led by Col. Edmund Scarburgh that was intended to wipe out the Pocomoke and Assateague Indians and pave the way for ownership by aspiring English settlers. Scarburgh was a powerful merchant-planter and surveyor from Accomack who had begun to accumulate properties throughout old Somerset County, Maryland. (Worcester County was subsequently divided from the seaside portion of Somerset County in 1742.) Scarburgh, a notorious Indian-hater, had convinced the governors of both Virginia and Maryland that the friendly Pocomokes and Assateagues were indeed hostile, and were an impediment to European colonization and the spread of Christianity. In fact, Scarburgh was simply one of the first land developers in the region.

In what has been referred to as the Seaside War, Scarburgh gathered an armed band of some 300 footmen with 60 horses to wipe out the Assateague Nation. The intent was clearly genocidal. Estimates of the number of casualties vary widely, but on the high side it was reported that Scarburgh's band had killed approximately 1,800 men, women, and children. Other accounts give a lower figure, citing the Indians' ability to slip off into the forests.

Scarburgh, along with smallpox, had become the severest of threats to the Assateagues. Any excuse sufficed to organize civilian vigilantes and lead armed charges into the Indian camps. By the time the Maryland Assembly eventually caught on to Scarburgh's tactics and had him removed from government councils, the damage was done.

The practice of displacing Indians from their traditional lands on the Lower Eastern Shore would become widespread by the late 1600s. This would be a pattern to be repeated time and again throughout the country. The fortunes of the Assateagues, along with the other Delmarva tribes, was inevitable. Foremost, perhaps, was the clash of cultures: Christian versus (in the European mind) savage; planter versus food-gatherer; light versus dark skin.

Another critical difference was in their concepts of land use. The English held a European view that land was the coin of the realm, and ownership of the land was the means to prosperity and happiness. The Indians, on the other hand, believed the land belonged to everyone—no fences, no signs. This was a much broader view of the use of open spaces than even what passed down today in the common law Public Trust Doctrine, which establishes public access to tidal waters, lakes, rivers, and streams in the United States.

This uneven view of public (Indian) versus private (English) rights would not be resolved. The Maryland Assembly made an attempt to intervene in the late 1600s. The Assembly fostered a policy of encouraging its predominately English constituency to cluster into settlements, with the intent of slowing down the rate at which the traditional Indian hunting grounds were being cut up into plantations and smaller farms. The policy didn't work then; it remains to be seen whether it will work today. Growth management and public versus private property rights have re-emerged as the seaside's foremost issues.

From 1660 to1680, Indian reservations were established on Delmarva both for the purpose of providing some compensation to the Indians for their lost lands and deprived rights—and, perhaps more importantly, to restrict their movements. Though the Delmarva Indians may have been a poorly-armed adversary, there was an ongoing concern among the settlers that the Iroquois Nations would descend from the Susquehanna River region, galvanize the local tribes, and drive the Europeans back into the sea. The Iroquois were anti-British, pro-French, and formidable warriors. Farfetched as such an attack may have been, it made a timely excuse to expropriate the traditional Indian hunting grounds.

Two reservations along the Pocomoke River, Askinimikansen and Queponqua (or Queponco), absorbed most of the Assateagues and Pocomokes in this, the first stage of the Indian diaspora. In the Indian dialect, Queponcua meant "ashes of pine woods at the limit of the sands." Askinimikansen is also translated with poetic license as "a stony place where they pick berries." Beautifully descriptive, yet somehow wistful, the names of these reservations seem to have carried premonitions of the future.

Another sequestration at Indian River in lower Delaware, Askekesky reservation, also absorbed some of the Assateagues (or Kickotanks) together with Nanticoke Indians from lower Delaware. The Assateagues may have been the remnants of the band located around St. Martin River behind Fenwick, where a century before the Indians had found Henry Norwood, nursed his stranded party back to health, and treated the survivors as visiting royalty.

The end of a significant Indian presence was at hand, and the reservations would close long before the eighteenth century was out. Beads of peak and roanoke could not support the dwindling Indian settlements, nor stave off duplicitous acquirers of the reservation lands. The fur trade, which had given the Indians some small leverage in a barter economy, had also collapsed, due in part to depleted numbers of the fur-bearer animals. A final treaty was pushed upon the Assateagues in 1742, which would assure that the remaining tribal members, for over 200 years to come, would be deprived of the rights of ordinary citizens. Now, fewer in number and dispossessed, the Assateague Indians dispersed, many following the path of other Indian tribes by heading north, to be taken in by the Iroquois.

Some of the Assateagues remained behind. The Mattaponi Indian Nation, currently headquartered in Virginia, claims ancestral ties to the Assateagues who migrated southward, at first hiding out in the marshes and swamps of the lower Delmarva Peninsula. Other Assateagues, probably among those who had been sequestered in the Indian River reservation, would assimilate into the local communities in lower Delaware, however best they could, sometimes joining with African-Americans. Here, the Assateague's history begins to cloud. The loss of basic rights and the stigma of Native American heritage kept the Assateagues, like many other Indian tribes, "in the closet." This was especially true in regions such as Delmarva, where non-whites were traditionally penalized.

In recent years, the renewed pride in Native American ancestry and culture sheds new light on these first inhabitants of the Maryland seaside. As the pendulum swings toward greater visibility, the challenge to the researcher is in sorting out the real from the ersatz, the genuine article from the wannabe.

Larry Smack, a.k.a Chief Medicine Cat (TP: 2004)

My grandfather, Elton D. Smack, started with me when I was about twelve years old. He might have been the last full-blooded Assateague Indian. He bragged about being Indian. My father didn't, but you have to remember what it had been like having Indian blood. Up until not too long ago an Indian couldn't own land, couldn't own a gun, couldn't travel anywhere he wanted, couldn't vote, couldn't get married in a Christian church. I couldn't even do my religious ceremony, Sun Dance, until 1972. Legally, I couldn't run a sweat lodge until 1972 either, unless you wanted to get hit with a $10,000 fine and time in jail. Federal law. You'd keep quiet, too. Anyway, we knew we had native blood, we just had to find it in us.

The turning point for me came when I was about twenty-one—I had my ups and downs before that—and I made my first visit to the sweat lodge, with the Creeks. Thought they were trying to kill me...most spiritual experience I ever had. Captain John Smith, when he traveled up the Chesapeake Bay, he called them sweat houses and he couldn't understand why the Indians would go jump in the bay or river after coming out of the sweat houses, no matter what time of year. But he didn't understand that we immersed our bodies in water every day. Spiritual.

Anyway, it was an overwhelming spiritual experience for me and that's when I began to walk the Red Path. You walk the White Path, see. 'Course the Bible says no matter which path you take, they all lead to the same place. Walking the Red Path, the Native Path, there's one word that describes it—conservation. The Spirit is in everything. You know, even when I chop down a tree I say a prayer over it, thank Mother Earth and the Creator, and then I wait until the next day, if I can, to come back and chop it down. And I apologize to it, the Spirit in it. Same kind of thing with an animal. If I shoot a deer for food, I take a young one, and I say the prayers over it.

That first experience in the sweat lodge gave me the hunger to learn. Well, I had already learned a few things from Grandfather, like making fish traps...and duck traps, hah! But I decided to take to the road and for seven years I visited the Leaders in other tribes, to learn the Native Way. When I started out, I was Chief Medicine Bear, but one of the Leaders, down south, told me, "You ain't no bear. You're a panther." So I became a panther until I came back up here and worked with the Nanticokes. They had a hard time saying the Indian word for panther, so we made it "Cat," which is what a panther is anyway, a big cat.

Back during that time I had a bad accident on my motorcycle, and it messed me up bad inside and out. To heal myself I went to live on Assateague for about three months. That was back before the bridge. I just took with me a few supplies I could carry, my teepee—I mean tent—a .22 rifle, some sugar, flour, that kind of stuff, and a bag of M&Ms. Everything else I lived off the land, you know, fish and clams and crabs. I shot a small sika. Prayed over it. Once a week, usually on Saturdays, I would take the ferry back to South Point to pick up a few supplies on the mainland. Jack "Pot Pie" who ran the ferry, he would know when to come pick me up. Yeah, I explored the Island from one end to the other, spent time around Green Run where my tribe had their summer camp, way back when. They moved to the mainland in the winter, over near the Pokomokes, what in our language were the "Muddy River People."

It was there on the Island that I had my first true vision, from the Elders, in the spiritual realm, who spoke to me in a language I could understand. Things happened to me that White Man wouldn't understand. I had visitors every night, ancestors.

Yeah, it bothers me, bothers me a lot, that all this is being covered up. Too many people. Development. Why, I could show you all kinds of places that were sacred to us, where you see a house covering it up now, or some kind of development. Did you know that the marina at Ocean Pines is sitting on top of one of our ossuaries? I tried to

> **complain, but it didn't do no good. I'll bet they would never have been allowed to build something on top of a White Man's graveyard.**
>
> **Two of my granddaughters are going along the Native Path. That's a good sign. Oh, and I forgot to say, our tribe didn't come over here from Asia on some bridge of ice. No sir, we don't have any Asian in us. DNA has proved that. Could be we came from somewhere else, and then again maybe we've always been here. That's something to think about.**

As the Assateague Indians were evacuated in such a remarkably short period of time, the English settlers quickly took their place, as inevitably as a rising tide on the full moon. Within a generation after Scarburgh's expedition—and the reported killing of many hundreds of seaside Indians—the lands along the seaside were surveyed, assigned to private owners, and divided into arable properties. Much of the advance work was now being done by the surveyor, Col. William Stevens, a wealthy merchant-planter from Rehoboth, in Somerset County, Maryland, whose name and land grants adorn many early county records.

The initial settling of the lower (Old) Somerset County came first, beginning in 1660, as most of the foot traffic was making its way northward from Virginia into Maryland. Soon, Stevens would come to Sinepuxent. In 1676, Stevens surveyed and took claim to an ideally situated tract of waterfront land to be titled as Genezar, which took up 2,200 acres at the south end of Sinepuxent Neck. This property was re-assigned, for a fee of course, to two Virginia buyers, whose families would remain connected with the property for the next 250 years. Goshen and Mayfields, large tracts lying contiguously to the north of Genesar, underwent similar transactions. Altogether, these properties extended over nearly ten miles of waterfront along the Sinepuxent and Newport Bays.

Here was the outpost of English civilization, based in the farmlands. It would take another hundred years for the seaside to refocus its development from an agrarian lifestyle to that of the emerging hamlets and villages with a commercially more diverse economy. Pocomoke, Snow Hill, and Trappe, followed by Berlin, grew out of this shift from plantation to settlement life. A general prosperity had brought about what policies and proclamations from the State General Assembly could not: a focus on growth into more secure and prospering communities. Families had multiplied and outgrown the carrying capacity of their forefathers' lands. The most opportune relocations were at the increasingly frequented crossroads along the overland north-south travel route—by now called the Philadelphia Post Road.

The new villages thrived—except for Trappe, which did not survive the early twentieth century—changing landscapes, some now invisible, but not lost to the keen observer.

Uncharted Waters during "First Contact"

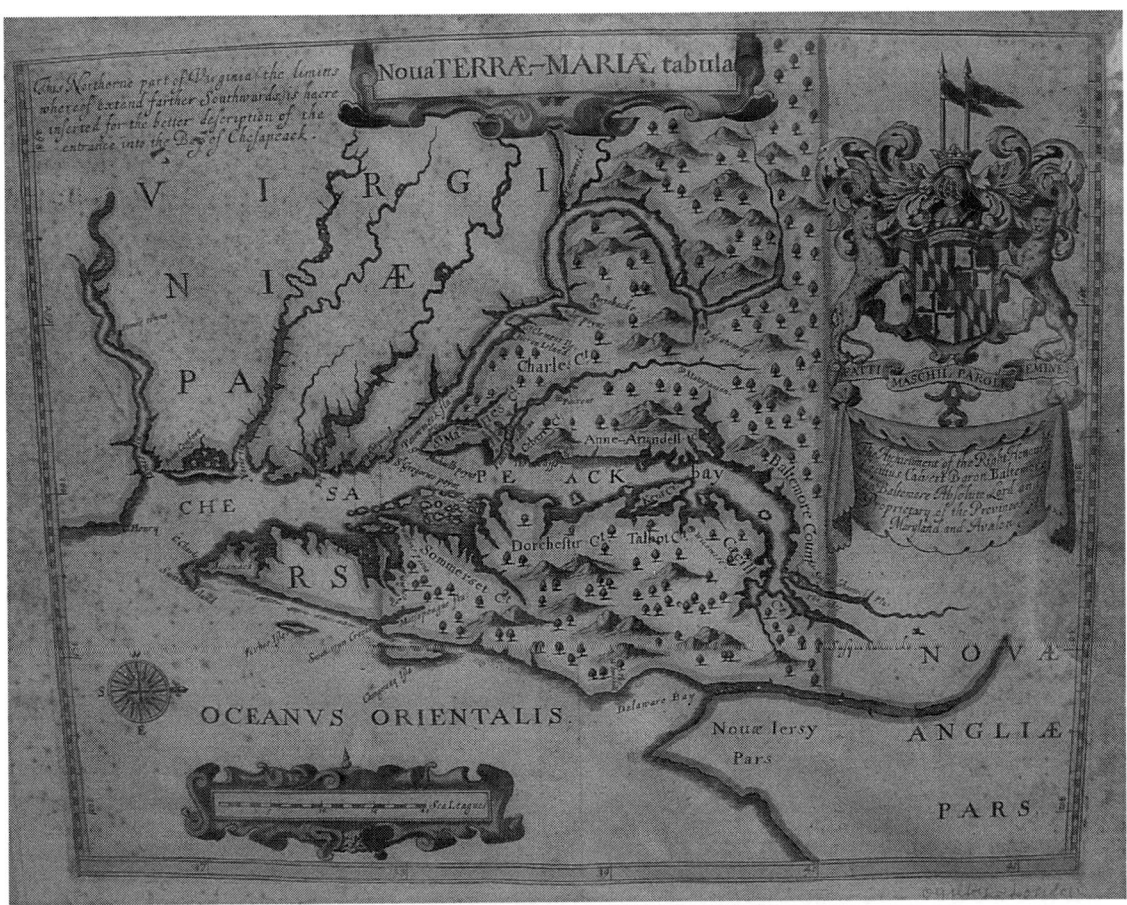

John Smith explored some 3,000 miles of the Chesapeake Bay and its tributaries in 1907-08, making initial contact with Native Americans. That his charted journeys did not include the seaside region is apparent: coastal bays are omitted. Yet, his mapping of the region as a whole served historians, explorers, and cartographers for the next hundred years. A subsequent map based on Smith's work was included with Lord Calvert's 1635 pamphlet for would-be colonizers. The pamphlet referred to local Indian tribes having been subdued through raids and massacres—possibly to allay concerns of the colonizers. Subsequent massacre of Assateague Indians would follow during the Seaside War.

A number of historical maps are contained in "The Hammond-Harwood Atlas of Historical Maps of Maryland, 1608-1908." The above map, typical of the Smith derivatives, is a 1671 original copy, signed "Ogilvy-London." (Collection of the author)

Uncovering the Past

Treasure-hunter Gene Parker pieces together an Assateague Indian pot gathered during an outing along the coastal bays. Such artifacts have yielded much of what is known about these Native Americans and the early colonists who replaced them.

Photo by the author

Medicine Cat

Dressed for Native American ceremonies at the local powwow…crafter of spirit sticks and pipes and teacher of Sacred Red Road Ways (left).

In Medicine Cat's right hand is a prehistoric healing pipe found along the Assawoman Bay. One end of the pipe would be pressed against the ailing area of the body, and the healer would inhale from the other end to draw out the evil spirits. In the left hand is a spirit stick, or staff, to protect the traveler from harm (below).

Photos by the author

V

A roof-top dove echoes that mournful coo,
"No one here, no one here, no one here."
Only the passing dog fox stops to hear,
and leaves his mark by the post and rail
just beneath the sign, "For Sale."

Colonial Architectural Gems: A Coastal Legacy in Jeopardy

England in the mid-seventeenth century was in turmoil. A stubborn and imperious monarch, Charles I, battled with puritanical, reform-minded Parliamentarians led by Oliver Cromwell. In 1649, Charles I was tried and executed, though the Cromwellian forces later gave way to supporters of Charles II who ascended the throne in 1660. Leading opponents of the monarchy quickly scattered like hunted animals, often losing themselves among the shiploads of New World-bound settlers. Certain well-known enemies of the Crown—at least, so a few imaginative genealogists have believed—would end up in the obscure backwoods, swamps, and isolated peninsulas of the Lower Eastern Shore of

Maryland and Virginia. Here, as in New England, they presumably reunited with their relatives and peers to form a new and flourishing landed gentry of merchant-planters.

A half-century later, a small influx of French Huguenots would also come to the Eastern Shore, seeking refuge following the revocation of the Edict of Nantes by King Louis XVI. Nearly 100 years of religious freedom that had been permitted to Protestants in a Catholic-dominated country had abruptly come to an end. Respectable French family names such as Brevard and Prideaux now mixed with their English counterparts—Rackliffes, Purnells, Whaleys, Henrys, et al— in a cordial, atypical display of historic Anglo-French relations.

The "forgotten" coastal bays of Maryland, particularly out of sight and out of the mind of the Kings' New World governors, present a view that repeats itself in each chapter of this region's history. Unlike the colonial past in the tidewater region of the Chesapeake Bay—more extensively documented as a center of commercial and political importance—Maryland's seaside remained apart from the social mainstream and the attention of many archivists. The first dwellings raised by settlers on the seaside, normally a reliable record of the way of life of the times, were usually modest wood-frame constructions that rarely withstood fire, storm, and rot for more than a few generations. More than a half-century of early settlement life passed by—dating from the massacre of the Assateague Indians in 1659 by Major Scarburgh's raiding parties—before a tangible picture of living along the coastal bays began to emerge.

Personal diaries, oral history, property records, and wills and testaments fill in part of this early tableau. But it would be the second generation of homes, now more substantial and often of fine brick construction, that would survive and help to interpret a golden age of plantation and rural farm life that emerged in the eighteenth and nineteenth centuries. These colonial dwellings are a mine of information to archeologists about the customs of the age. Buried in the surrounding grounds are centuries of discarded kitchen utensils, farm implements, and children's toys that add to this picture of coastal life. The artifacts, superseding the earlier footprints of Native Americans, reinforce an image of the independent "merchant"-planter engaged both in commerce as well as farming the land.

The notable homes remaining from this period also tell a story of relatively affluent living, at least by those owners of large tracts of arable land. Despite mosquito-borne fevers, occasional crop failures, hurricanes, and British blockades of their shipping trade, the families and followers of these first merchant-planters continued to grow and prosper. Nowhere in the county is this more evident than in Sinepuxent Neck. A handful of time-weathered structures, here and across Trappe Creek on Newport Farm, are considered the most important group of early American homes along the entire coastal bays, if not the entire state.

However, not unlike the fate of the earliest wood-frame homes, this more substantial tidewater architectural heritage is in jeopardy. Not from untended wood stoves, or termites, or flimsy construction, rather having been cast aside by the relentless creep of residential development spreading south from Ocean City to satisfy the yearnings to live as close by the sea as possible. Still, the past, present, and future are all here in a compact zone that may be reached from Route 611 and South Point Road, or by boat along a parallel water-trail.

Five outstanding historic dwellings stand between the main road and the bay shoreline, traveling from Frontier Town amusement park and campground toward South Point. From north to south the list begins with the Fassitt House, one of the two oldest remaining waterside homes in northern Worcester County. These properties may be accessed with the owners' permissions, and may also be opened for periodic garden tours.

The Fassitt House was built in 1730 by Capt. William Fassitt, one of the earliest property holders in Sinepuxent, dating to the late 1600s—about the time the Assateague Indians were being pushed from their traditional bayside hunting and fishing grounds to inland reservations. The Fassitt House is situated away from the water's edge—unlike construction practices today—and is now barely visible from Sinepuxent Bay. The house features outstanding Flemish-bond masonry, dark-glazed header bricks with fanciful diamond and zigzag patterns, and is considered one of the finest examples of its kind in the Mid-Atlantic region.

Capt. Fassitt was a planter, sea vessel owner, and an early follower of the Reverend Francis Makemie, the pioneer of Presbyterianism in the colonies. According to one legend, pirates captured Fassitt's vessel off Fenwick Island, tied up his crew, and were chaining Fassitt when he cried out piteously, "Do anything you want to, boys, only don't throw me overboard—the water's full of sharks!" The pirates promptly heaved him overboard. In the water he was as much at home as Br'er Rabbit in the briar patch and swam safely to the beach, making his way home to his Sinepuxent estate. The same tale is also attributed to one of William Fassitt's sons, Captain James Fassitt. Whether by coincidence or determinant DNA, many of Capt. Fassitt's progeny in future generations would be legendary swimmers, and tales of their prowess abound.

Ned Carey, a commercial waterman and recent resident of the Fassitt House, is a direct descendent of Capt. Fassitt, signifying the enduring family ownership of waterfront properties along the coastal bays. Family continuity has also been the case at Henry's Grove. Here, the Julia Henry House was built in 1792 by John Fassitt, great grandson of Capt. William Fassitt, who had taken residence on the adjacent tract nearly a century before. The property subsequently passed into the neighboring Henry family (hence Henry's Grove), then in the twentieth century to their McCabe cousins, and currently on to Hale Harrison, a prominent Ocean City hotelier with links to this rambling family tree.

The Julia Henry House commands a visible presence along the Sinepuxent Bay, etched against a background of tidewater farmland and distinguished by its exceptional, well-preserved Georgian-style brick architecture. According to the commonplace local legend, its prominence invited a shelling from British warships that entered the bay through the Sinepuxent Inlet during the War of 1812. It is also alleged that at least one cannonball struck the home and that others were recovered over time in the surrounding fields. Similar claims are proudly made for other properties along the coastal bays. Apparently, an armed British craft entered the bay in 1813 through the former Sinepuxent Inlet searching for food to supply the blockading British fleet. From the number of reported cannon blasts that resound in local accounts, it could have been the work of an armada.

The nearness of the main residence to the water's edge, uncommon among the more safely sited homes of the period, may have had much to do with John Fassitt's strategy of keeping a watchful eye on Assateague Island. Fassitt, a notorious scavenger of vessels floundering in the surf, could survey the beach scene from the vantage point of his upstairs bedroom. He might then have been the first to pounce on distressed cargo.

Alone of the extant older homes along the Sinepuxent Bay, Williams Grove, built in 1810, is wood-framed, as compared to the usually more enduring construction of locally-fired brick. The home retains its cypress shingle exterior, a trademark of early homes in the area due to the available supplies of cypress from the Pocomoke swamp and, along the coastal bays, at Shingle Landing Prong. Another feature is the "telescope" profile of the dwelling, each section presenting a new elevation. This is a distinct architectural style of the Federal Period on the Lower Eastern Shore. According to one report, the dwelling was first shared as a tavern for the shipping trade, using the passage through Sinepuxent Inlet and the then-deepwater landing on the property. Vessels sailed away laden with lumber, tobacco, and farm produce. Ships would return with cargoes of limestone, for processing into lime in the local kilns, and with manufactured goods that may well have included silk dresses for wear at the Sinepuxent Christmas balls and sporting outfits suitable for the fox hunts and horse races that had become favorite pastimes among the landed aristocracy.

It's hard to think of horse races today on Rt. 611, when the traffic bound for the Assateague parks is bumper to bumper on the steamy days of July and August. But let the traffic clear out after Labor Day and the weather cool, and one can imagine a well-padded dirt lane in front of Williams Grove that connected the estates in Sinepuxent Neck. Imagine, too, the end of a week when harvests were packed in, the ships loaded for distant ports, and the ladies dressed for the occasion. Leisure time in the country had its pleasures.

Today, the Williams Grove house is visible from the bay, located just behind a prominent red boathouse and flanked by attractive waterside properties of more recent vintage. Mr. and Mrs. Ricks Savage are the current owners of Williams Grove.

Of course, there was undoubtedly another side to life on the farm that belonged to the field hands and tenant workers.

> **Backwoods Life in Sinepuxent**
> **Alfred Showell (NPS: 2001)**
>
> One man was named Charlie Brown. He was the biggest whiskey maker around. He was a nice, old, grown man, too, he was. Boy, he made some whiskey, I mean, him and his men. He was a white guy—many whites as they was blacks. You know somethin' else? You know where Sinepuxent is, don't you? Yeah, that woods all down there, back in there, that's where they have the whiskey stills. Yes, sir. Well, I tell you the truth, I don't see how a bootlegger ever got by like he did. You go in the woods, you hear that thing puffin' and blowin' almost the whole woods when they're running whiskey, you know. When they're cookin' it, yes indeed, for you could hear it to plain, you know. You could be walkin' through the woods, you hear it, hear that thing runnin'.

A mile down the road, the Rackliffe House property (a.k.a. the Dirickson Farm, or Sandy Point Farm) is currently owned by the State of Maryland and prominently situated just southwest of the Verrazano Bridge. A section of the house was built initially in 1752 by Charles Rackliffe, a descendent of the ancestral Charles Rackliffe, one of two original grantees of the property dating to 1678. A generation after this first construction, portions of the house burned in a fire that may have been set by a British raiding party during the Revolutionary War.

Adversity happened again when this modified, stuccoed-over brick building was gutted by fire in 1928—ignited, it was rumored, by a secretly-operated still. This may have been possible, for this once-grand home was now in the unsupervised hands of tenants. The last resident-owner, James Bravard Dirickson, died in 1902, a year after Queen Victoria, and here, too, an era had ended. Family owners had occupied the plantation house for 150 years, but never again. Dirickson, a bachelor throughout his lifetime, engaged a household of black tenants, including Martha Hargrow, a young mulatto farm laborer who was Dirickson's housekeeper and caregiver—and presumably his mistress. In his will, Dirickson divided off a small farm on the north side of the property and left it to Martha. This portion was called Little Sandy Point Farm.

In the repairs after the 1928 fire, a new, hip roof replaced the original gabled roof, and certain interior changes further altered the building design—diminishing the aesthetic and historic values of the property.

The dwelling has remained uninhabited since 1991 and has substantially deteriorated since being vacated—ravaged by vandals and smothered by ivy. Nevertheless, a rescue may be at hand. Rackliffe House Trust, a nonprofit foundation, is applying to lease the property from the Maryland Department of Natural Resources with plans to restore the structure to its original colonial appearance. When restoration is completed, Rackliffe House will be opened to the public as a museum, with the purpose of interpreting the plantation heritage of this and other surrounding colonial sites. As such, this may be the only ocean-facing plantation house with public access located along the Mid-Atlantic coast.

The Rackliffe House will also be remembered as the most notable "haunt" in the county. The ghost stories are legend—and not simply the wide-eyed tales of youngsters, but remarkably correlating reports from a succession of well-educated tenants with professional livelihoods. An investigation of the poltergeists was published in the *Maryland Coast Press* (forerunner of *The Dispatch*), the weekly edition of April 22, 1983, under the heading, "A Worcester Haunting—One thing is certain: 'There's something in that house.'" The article describes eyewitness accounts of the many strange supernatural occurrences, such as repeated instances of framed pictures on the walls being turned upside down and backwards in their frames without any evidence of tampering. Curtains have been found, upon morning awakening, removed from the walls and carefully stowed at right angles to the wall and window from which they were removed. Sounds of music, shuffling of feet, and the faint scent of perfume wafting from the area of the old ballroom floor have also been regular events, to say nothing of the painful sighs and howls in the night.

The hauntings have been attributed to various incidents in the past. One is laid to Charles Rackliffe, who had a reputation for mistreating his plantation slaves. According to legend, Rackliffe's "negro men sprang upon him in his own lane and murdered him." This supposedly gives credence to the howls in the night. Another tale describes the misadventures of a woman, presumably the Lady of the House, who had just dressed for a gala dance—and died when she fell coming down the stairs. Her ghost carries whiffs of perfume and the sound of faint strands of music and the shuffling of dancing feet in the middle of the night.

Denise Milko (TP: 2005)

Rackliffe House was my childhood home. At that time many local people called it the Rum Point Haunted House, and sometime earlier it had been known as Sandy Point Dancing Floor House because of all the parties that used to take place there. It has an incredible history. The house is sitting on former Indian camping grounds. Legend also has it that a cannonball went through the side of the house during the War of 1812. But it was the strange happenings when I lived there that I will always remember.

At night, the horses in the barn would sometimes go crazy, usually when we would also hear the voices in the night. The tenants down the road said the voices were just puppy frogs—they probably meant tree frogs—yet these were clear voices, sometimes along with the crying of a baby....and then the piano downstairs would start playing by itself. One night we were sitting around the dinner table with friends, and one friend, Gene Parker, said emphatically, "I don't believe in ghosts." Just then all the lights in the house went off and the candles flared up. Ask him about it.

> One of my scariest moments came when I heard the long, weighty, glass window shatter downstairs, as though someone was breaking in the house. Then came some gun shots and dogs barking. I called the police and then my parents, who were out for the evening. When they arrived, there were no signs of broken glass nor of any person or animal having come on the property. After this, I slept out in the family room for the next year. I know this all sounds a little weird, but it wasn't just in my imagination. We had several older aunts who would come and stay with us. Once, when we left them alone, they went through similar experiences and actually fled the house.
>
> I think whatever, or whoever it may have been, wanted to scare me at first. But I didn't have any real fear of the supernatural or the occult. So if there were spirits there, I think they finally decided to leave me alone. Later, when doing some research on the history of Rackliffe House, I went to St. Paul's church cemetery in Berlin—which I hadn't been through before—to visit grave sites of all the people buried there who had been connected with Rackliffe House. And something very eerie happened. It was if someone took me by the hand and led me directly to each exact grave among the hundreds of other burial sites in the cemetery. It was unnerving.

"Rising sheer, gaunt, and bare, but strangely appealing...most noted of all the houses on Sinepuxent Neck," was the description in 1940 by one historian viewing the vacated and already-deteriorating dwelling known as Genesar. The name Genesar (in its several variations) may be derived from the rare Douay version of the *Bible*, St. Matthew 14:34.

The dwelling is still there, battling the elements of deterioration, partially hidden from South Point Road by foliage, and seemingly incongruous among surrounding new construction. Its slim and simple elegance, an extraordinary expression of the so-called Transitional Style, stands in contrast to the boxy and rambling dwellings that would follow. Genesar's high, narrow two-and-a-half story structure is further described as virtually "leaping upward from the flat coastal plains." The handsome glazed-brick pattern, though heavily weathered at this point, has been cited as the most outstanding example of its kind in

Maryland, if not the United States. This exterior brick work shares some of the features of the Fassitt House, which was built at about the same time, suggesting that the two most prestigious dwellings in Sinepuxent Neck may have been designed by the same person.

Tenant Life on Genesar in 1920
Luvinia Spence & Hazel Holland—Sisters (NPS: 2004)

There was more than one teni's house. There was Genezar. That was the main house. That was the slave house back then. We used to find arrows...as kids playin'. They used to be Indians had that place before my father got there, maybe before Dr. Zadok (Dr. Zadok Purnell Henry III). I guess he inherited the farm. And he had Hickory Farm, named Dirickson (Rackliffe) Farm, maybe six houses, yeh, Straw House and one in de woods. Hickory House that we stayed in, everyone wanted to look at it...They come down to look at the fireplace 'cause the fireplace was big enough for a man to walk in. You can walk in and stand up in the fireplace, and we use some kind of iron to hold up these great big pots, we call 'em hog tub pots. Dat's what dey cooked by. You had no kind of stoves to cook on, so they used to make bread, put it in the fireplace to cook it. And then they got smart enough that when dey wanted baked potatoes, dey put the potatoes in ashes.

Oh, dey were tough times. I remember my father...there was a man hired him to work, paid him ten cents an hour. That was money, wasn't it? And if you had a horse, and you weren't using it, you'd rent it, like a man. That was twelve cent for de horse and ten cents for de man. Dey good time. Good time. I wish I could go back. Gooder time than now. I wisht I could go and know what I know now. I'd be a happy woman.

It was a one-room school (for African Americans), I'm think now it had to be a twenty by twenty...maybe, but it wasn't big. It had four windows, two windows on each side of the stove. Yeah, burnt wood. And then you'd freeze to death. It was so cold, by the time you got to school your hands were numb. I think goin' back as far as I know, I

> think those grades didn't go much further than third. I'll tell you, Genezar School was the lowest grade school in the world 'cause kids didn't go to school. Lots of times this teacher would be in school by herself, an' most of the kids might stay home and work.
>
> We had a Santie Claus come to us every year. We had to go to bed for the night and wait for Santie Claus to come. We'd get up thinkin' we have nothin' on our plate. (But) we had a little candy, orange, or apple, somethin' like that. We didn't get no toy at that time, you just get some candies and stuff. Sometime might get a little doll baby...And we go 'round to other people's houses, hollerin', "Christmas gift, Christmas gift," and they give us candy and some oranges if they have 'em and they come to our home and we give 'em de same.

Genesar may be considered the initial seed in the settling of lands along the Neck. The property was assigned to Charles Rackliffe and Edward Wale in 1678, although a portion was subsequently divided off to Rackliffe. The Genesar home, as it now stands (there was probably an earlier frame structure on or near the same location), was built by Major John Purnell and his wife, Elizabeth Rackliffe, about 1732. The owners, Mr. and Mrs. Don Humphrey, have spent much of the last thirty years seeking support for the building's restoration. Mr. Humphrey recently passed away in 2004.

In addition to the architectural interest of Genesar, the property carries with it a fascinating tale involving one of the two first landowners, Edward Wale. Was he, in fact, Edward Whalley, cousin of Oliver Cromwell and one of the regicide judges who collectively sentenced England's King Charles I to death? Whalley, reputedly one of the most skilled swordsmen in England, served as an officer under the parliamentarian Cromwell against the Royalists. With the defeat of Cromwell's Roundheads and the accession of Charles II to the throne, Whalley fled to New England. A tradition in the local Whalley family (one "l") has it that Whalley, still being pursued by the King's agents, escaped to the Eastern Shore of Virginia and later found refuge in Sinepuxent Neck under the assumed name of Wale. Historians have disproved this account and provided good evidence that Whalley died while a fugitive in New England. However, there are also indications that Whalley and Wale may have been connected in some way. Father and son, or cousins? Herein lies a fascinating chapter of local colonial history that has yet to be concluded.

While weighing the arguments on either side of the Whalley yarn, a visitor to the property should stand by one of the outer walls, run a hand across the crevassed old bricks held together in the pocked interstices by crumbling mortar, and feel a shiver along the spine that comes involuntarily in the physical presence of antiquities resounding with echoes of the past. Then may the visitor read the notes from a diary written by one of the coterie of the first Presbyterian ministers on Delmarva, traveling from property to property and preaching the gospel, probably much like Seventh Day Adventists do today.

In describing the visit to South Point, the diarist drew a memorable picture of the aging squire: "My attention is attracted from everything else to an old gentleman...much worn with age and care; certainly 70 years or more, but there is a stateliness and dignity about him which is very marked. He is clad in a faded costume of the days of the Protector and bears himself with a military air reminding us of the soldiers of England...He looks like a man of grand experience, one used to command...I saw that grand old face beam with expression and the soul within seemed to arouse like a lion from sleep when one of the company brought up the subject of the then political situation in England...In a few days the same party touched the shores of South Point to put the Indian guide ashore and they saw, in the denser hummocks, the venerable old man walking thoughtfully, erect and slow, but if he noticed us at all it was to retire further into the recesses of the grove...Often have I thought of the venerable old man on the plantation of Genesar, whose dignity and military bearing so impressed me at the house of Mr. Wale."

One translation of Genesar has been ascribed as, "Here I rest." If accurate, the original owner, whoever he was, chose well.

Along this trail of architectural treasures, the visitor has been a witness to the land that Verrazano, the explorer, called Arcadia. The landscape changed little for the next 350 years, except for the clearing and planting of fields and the appearance of scattered homes and tenants' quarters. Then, in 1939 two brothers and a sister of the Henry family, who had inherited much of Sinepuxent from their forebearers, sold all their holdings for $96,131, which included eight and one-half miles of waterfront land on the Sinepuxent and Newport Bays. Today, a single two-acre waterfront lot fetches many times this amount.

Franklyn Woodcock, a partner of Lamar Corporation, had been assigned personal ownership of the Sinepuxent Neck lands and had promptly resold several of the parceled farms for a windfall profit, though holding on to the Genesar and the Rackliffe properties. In his real estate prospectus, "Synepuxent 1679 1939," Woodcock proclaimed at length the virtues of ownership of property in this Arcadia, and summarized what buyers would get for their money:

"An estate, in which you will be justly proud.

"An estate, accessible to the larger Eastern centers.

"An estate, which will bring health and happiness to the entire family, through the excellence of its climate, accessibility to both to both bay and ocean, and its advantages in hunting and riding.

"An estate, which is highly productive in both agricultural products and seafood.

"An estate, which should, and no doubt will, enhance materially with the years.

"An estate, which is practically self-contained, regardless of national or international economic and social conditions."

Realtors are still pitching some of the same sales points, even as these original estates have been whittled down into many pieces. As of this writing, one of the last open spaces in the original Genesar tract is under development, some 370 acres of tidewater forest and fields and marshes and a nearly perfect example of a Delmarva bay, that circular indentation in the land filled with ground water and rimmed with persimmon trees, pines, red oaks, and a low, tangled barrier of groundsel. New homes are arising in the shadow of the historic brick dwelling, which, even in its dilapidated condition, outshines its neighbors.

Fassitt House

Fassitt House (1730), the senior dwelling in Sinepuxent Neck, is among the dwindling number of colonial homes facing the coastal bays. The house has been modified several times. The roof and upstairs, which burned in 2003, have since been repaired. The exceptional Flemish-bond brickwork remains in good condition.

Photo taken in 1950, collection of Ned Carey

Henry's Grove

In 1792, John Fassitt moved into his new brick home, later known variously as Henry's Grove and later as Bayside Pony Farm. Here, Fassitt was able to look across the Sinepuxent Bay and scan the surf on Assateague Island. He was a scavenger of stranded vessels—most noteworthy being his looting of many hogsheads of gin from the foundered British ship *Lively*.

The dwelling exterior has been stabilized and maintained by current owner Hale Harrison.

Photo by author, 2004

Williams Grove

Ricks Savage, master story-teller, and wife Diane Savage, ardent preservationist, have cared well for their 1810 Williams Grove property. Also known as the Benson House, after previous owners, the wood-framed residence with its telescope profile is a singular 19th century bayside example of this once-popular traditional style.

Photo by author, 2004

Rackliffe House

Rackliffe House (1752) became known as Dirickson House in the late 19th and early 20th centuries, and after the 1940s as the Woodcock Farm. Its legendary history includes razing by British forces during the Revolutionary war, the murder of its first owner, a second near-fatal fire, ill-chosen architectural modifications, latter-day fame as the most notable haunted house in the country, and a recent period of neglect and deterioration.

In 1928, the roof and upper story of Rackliffe House were destroyed by fire. A hip roof replaced the original gabled roof, significantly altering the structure's appearance and architectural integrity. Tenants maintained the property from 1930-1991.

How quickly vacant propertied turn to ruins—the home choked with vines and the historic dairy a victim of a fallen tree.

Rackliffe House Trust, a nonprofit foundation formed in 2004, is planning to restore the property to its original appearance to serve as a public center for interpreting the cultural heritage of the coastal bays.

Photo 1904: collection of the author (top); Photo by the author, 1988 (middle); Photo by the author, 2004 (bottom)

Genesar

One of the most noted examples of the Transitional Style in the United States, Genesar marks the beginning of colonial plantation ownership along the coastal bays. More than an architectural study, Genesar echoes with stories of near-mythic proportion. The site calls for heritage preservation.

Mr. and Mrs. Don Humphrey have owned and cared for Genesar during the past half-century. Don Humphrey is now deceased, the future of Genesar undetermined.

Photo circa 1930: courtesy of National Park Service (middle); Photo by the author, 2004 (bottom)

Heritage Sites: Sinepuxent & Newport Bays

1. 1732 Genesar House
2. 1752 Rackliffe House
3. 1810 Williams Grove House
4. 1792 Henry's Grove House
5. 1730 Fassitt House
6. 18th Century Golden Quarter Farm
7. 1820 George Purnell House
8. Early 19th Century Lime Kiln & Farm House
* 9. 18th -19th Century Sea Port
* 10. Assateague Indian Trading Post
* 11. Assateague Indian Campground
* 12. Assateague Indian Ossuary
* 13. Early 18th Century Saltworks
* 14. Historic Shipwreck location

* Exact sites not available

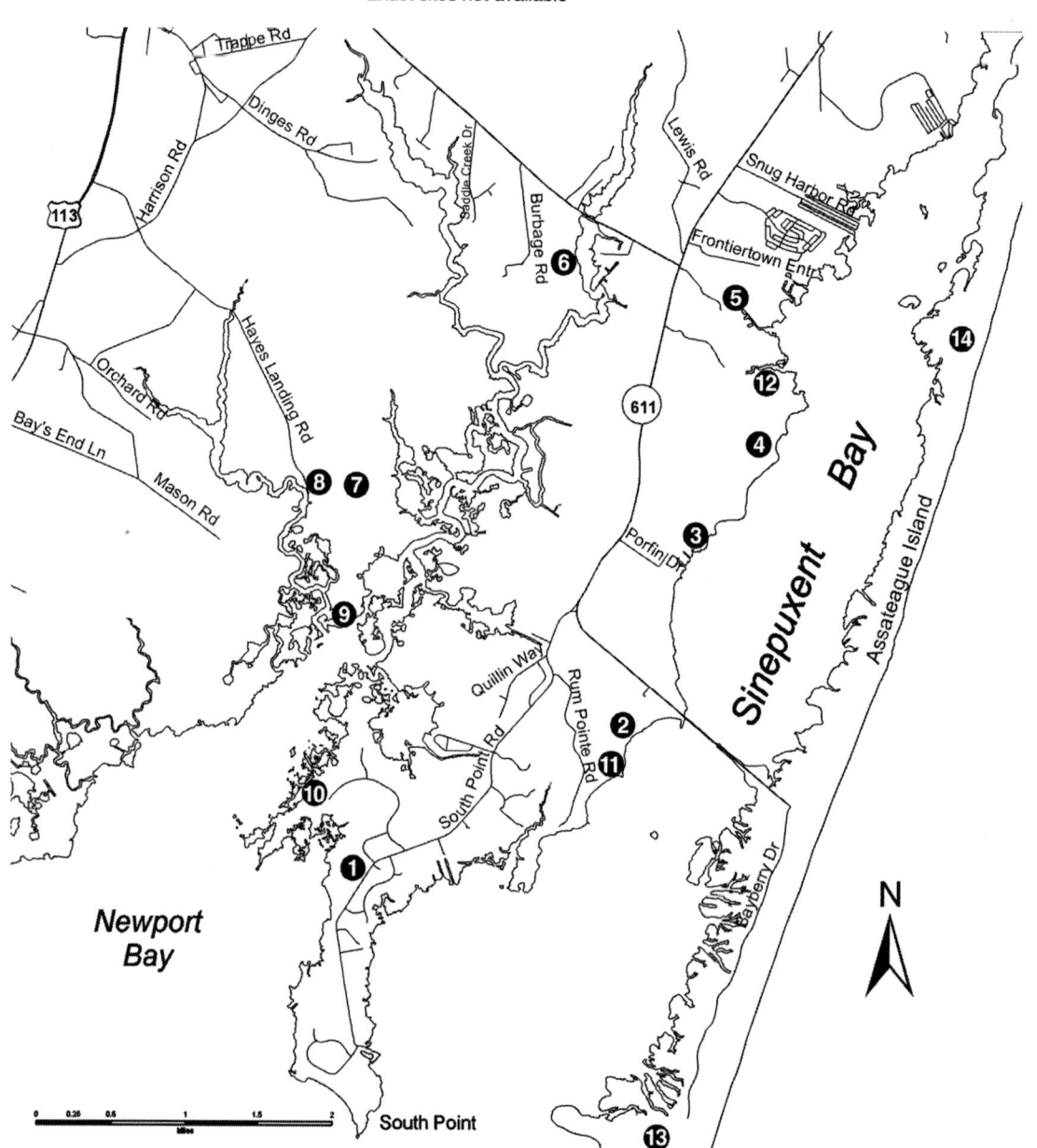

VI

Nothing is forever, for whatever loss;
yet cycles do repeat on that Island Across;
"I'm back, I'm back," is the two-note cry
of a cloud of honkers in the western sky,
with their wings locked on Assateague.

Island Settlements of the Past

One sure bet about Assateague Island has been that nothing here has been permanent: whether shorelines, dunes, inlets, or, especially, human settlement. The Assateague Indians must have gazed from the mainland with mixed feelings of awe and caution at "The Place Across."

Notwithstanding the food-gathering opportunities for the Indians during benevolent seasons, the harsher weather gods would send swarms of mosquitoes and black and greenhead flies over the island with a stifling land breeze during the dog days of July and August, and then chase away the soothing Indian summer of October with wintry blasts of nor'west winds. In these unkind times of the year the Indians would retreat from temporary outposts by the sea and find safe harbor in more permanent camps along the sheltered tributaries of Maryland's coastal bays. Fast forward to the present time and there is still a cycle of come and go, as visitors bathe and camp and fish and hunt in each particular season, then largely leave the island to nature's ways.

Yet, it is in between the first human era of Native Americans and latter-day surf-seekers that the most dogged efforts were made to domesticate Assateague. In a span of more than two hundred years, a number of attempts were made to create substantial settlements. The first English settlers putting down roots on Assateague Island were among the second wave of migrants to the seaside, who scrambled to find unclaimed lands not already granted to the earlier merchant-planters on the mainland. Daniel Jennifer is believed to have been the first landowner, having been granted in 1678 that portion of the island lying in Virginia. Subsequently, in 1711, Captain William Withington took up 1,000 acres around Green Run, becoming the first Marylander to own a piece of Assateague. Optimistic about the prospects for farming the thin sandy soils, Withington went on to claim and patent much of the entire barrier beach. In one of the land transactions during this period, 3,500 acres of the island were acquired for a price of 10,000 pounds of tobacco. While this sounds like a hefty price for that time, another report from a few years earlier indicates that Anthony Johnson, from Accomack, Virginia, sold "one maire coult" to a Francis Payne for 2,000 pounds of tobacco. By this count, a sizable portion of Assateague Island was valued at that of five young horses.

The island settlers who followed began to form into clustered enclaves by the end of the eighteenth century, and their small communities managed to survive into the early twentieth century based on farming the arable portions, grazing livestock on the marshlands, guiding parties of waterfowl hunters, and harvesting fish and oysters from the surrounding waters.

Norman Jones, Born on Assateague in 1913 (NPS: 1972)

Nobody had an icebox or a refrigerator and almost everybody was very religious. Nobody did anything on Sundays 'cept sing. Our parents would cook the Sunday meal

on Saturday. And in the summertime we would keep our food from spoiling, as soon as it got on Assateague, it would be cooked and put up trees in a large basket with a lid. And in the tree there would be more air. Most of our food was seafood. There was a lot of molasses and beans brought over from the mainland.

(As a boy of 13-14 years old)...If the tide weren't down enough to get some clams, he went to help his father to hoe the corn, work in that garden, get the grass out of it. In summertime you could wear an old pair of shoes and an old pair of trousers and go out up to your belt raking clams....After we got through clammin', there's a place up here on the beach called the swimming hole. We went up there, stripped off and swum for half an hour. 'Course in September most of us went back to school, and Saturday mornings every fella out there that could cut a piece of wood...he'd go help his father get wood. They wanted a lot of wood and store it to their woodpile so they woke up some mornin', the ground covered with snow, they didn't have to go out there in the woods, it was right there almost to the door block. And we were (cutting wood) from last of October until right up close to Christmas, gettin' all the wood that people wanted and see that the church and schoolhouse had enough wood to last 'em. After a while I remember that it was the talk of the little village up here the state's going to give us two ton o' coal so we could keep a fire over the weekend, so all these children won't have to get up...go down to build a fire. Well, my father sent me down there many a time. "Go down and build that fire...you stay right there...and don't let too much blaze go up the chimley."

Settlement life was dictated by virtual isolation, even from the adjacent mainland, and by a constant lookout for providential changes in the weather. The "elements" produced a tough and independent breed of people, some of whose descendants are the "Teaguers" of adjacent Chincoteague Island today. Strong Anglican names like Savage, Reed, Jester, Watson, Russell, and Mason have signified solid Eastern Shore stock. The principal communities were located at the southern tip of Assateague, in Virginia, and another at Green Run, the site of one of the former inlets situated about halfway between the Verrazano Bridge and the southern tip of the island. Smaller colonizations were situated around Pope Island, next to the Maryland-Virginia line, and another adjacent to the historic Sinepuxent Inlet at the southern end of North Beach.

Birch's salt works were located beside the Sinepuxent Inlet—an enterprise established by the Baltimore Salt Company during the Revolutionary War and flourishing during the British blockade of maritime trade, which continued intermittently through the War of 1812. The salt produced from the evaporation of seawater was essential to the preservation of food for local colonists as well as for supplies to the new country's militia.

While the families on Assateague during the late 1700s and 1800s must have been pressed to scratch out a bare living, they were nonetheless able to build a school and church to serve, for a time, a growing population. An early enterprise of the island settlers was the scavenging of ships that wrecked along the beach. This became such a issue that the Maryland Assembly appointed a wreck-master in 1790. The wreck-master's duty was to send deputies to the scene to protect the wreck from the local predators, so that the owners or their insurance agents could rescue the cargo. The Assembly also decreed that looters of vessels in distress, when the plundering could have contributed to the shipwreck, would be put to death summarily without benefit of clergy.

Another industry for the islanders was the recovery of the bodies of the drowned, shipwrecked sailors who washed ashore in those early days. The authorities paid at the rate of one pound for the finding and burial of each body. This windfall, too, would not last. The number of shipwrecks was reduced, beginning in the 1830s, when the first lighthouse was built on the island at Assateague Point in Virginia. Prices on the island could still be compared to the value of a few ponies: 50 acres of land were purchased by the government for the lighthouse for $439.99 and the structure was built and equipped for an additional $7,500. In another thirty years, just after the Civil War, the lighthouse was rebuilt for $75,000. Inflation had finally come to Assateague.

In 1871, the federal government also initiated further plans to reduce the loss of lives from shipwrecks by establishing the Life-Saving Service. Within a few years, life-saving stations were built at intervals along the coast. Four stations existed at one time or another on Assateague Island—at North Beach (at the location of the former Sinepuxent Inlet), Green Run, Pope Island, and at Assateague Point, near the southern tip of the island in Virginia. However, when the Life-Saving Service was converted into the U.S. Coast Guard in 1915, the stations lost their significance and were decommissioned over time. Gone are all the original stations, lost to storm or fire. However, the U.S. Coast Guard station at Assateague Point was reconstructed in 1922 on a new location by Tom's Cove and served the Coast Guard until being decommissioned in 1967. The building is now the property of the Park Service—its future use in question.

Milton Cooper (TP: 2004)

I had some great years down there at Pope's Island (Coast Guard) Station. That's where I went in, enlisted, 1935. Whew, I'm ninety years old now. Seen some good shootin' down there in them marshes. The game wardens had a hard time comin' across the marsh to get us. They used to ride up and down the beach, from Ocean City to Chincoteague. You could do that then....They'd come by the station about 5 o'clock (in the afternoon) and somebody would say, "Here he comes. Get ready, boys." By the time they passed the station headed south we had our boots on to go out for some night shootin'.

I used to do all my fishing right out in front of the station. We used to eat at 4 o'clock, and afterward I'd go over beach fishin'. I've got as high as five drum after supper. In spring the fish would bring anywhere from 18 to 20 pound. They were smaller drum. In the fall they'd run from 35 to 50 pound. Good times.

Duty as "surfmen" with the Life-Saving Service is a legendary part of the history of Assateague Island. These were hardy men, strong swimmers, toughened from patrolling the beach on foot and handling their heavy clinker-built dories in rough surf. Many lived a lonely life, leaving family on the mainland and, on occasion, making visits home during their off-time. Other surfmen moved their families onto the island, building shanties near the station and becoming part of the Assateague community. For all this, they were paid $20 a month with room and board.

Another of Assateague's once-bustling enterprises was Scott's Ocean Beach House, built just north of Green Run in 1869. Before the resort of Ocean City existed, Scott's was the premier, and only, beachfront hotel to cater to sportsmen during the fall-to-spring gunning season and to vacationers during the summer season, who would come for the fresh sea air, carriage rides on the beach, and the groaning tables of local Eastern Shore fare. The Ocean Beach House was also popular with the clergy, on retreats, and with newlyweds, closeting themselves in the private cottage annex next door. The hotel could accommodate from forty to fifty guests, whose journey to the beach would require various modes of transportation: starting with a trip by stagecoach or, after 1876, by the new railroad through Snow Hill, then taken by liverymen to Public Landing on Chincoteague Bay, and finally sailing across the bay to Scott's Landing at Green Run aboard the *Fairfield*, Captain Frederick Connor's two-masted sailing rig.

Don Bowden, Sr. (NPS: 1978)

My father's grandfather was named Scott and he had a hotel on the beach... now commonly known as Green Run. Then it was named Middlemoor. This only building (Scott's Ocean Beach House) was a long hotel. It was three stories high, about thirty rooms long and a porch ran the length of the building on each floor. And rich people from the cities like Boston, New York, Philadelphia would come down and do game

> hunting, wild duck, and in the summer they would come channel bass fishing. Very wealthy people. My grandfather would have people to meet them in a sailboat and take 'em across the bay, and they would have a buckboard...a buckboard is operated with two horses and it has a flat body and about four seats that two people can sit abreast. My father when he was small would go up and be bus boy and wait on people. It had pool tables and it had a telephone, which was a rarity for someplace like that. After my father's grandfather died and the family left, storms tore the building down. People stopped using the beach.
>
> Then after we moved to Chincoteague, there were two ways to get off the island. There was a black boat and a white boat. Allie Jester ran the white boat and the Collins brothers ran the black boat, and they were docked right next to each other. They were fine people but were competition to each other. They went from Chincoteague to Franklin City to carry people to the train.... People would pack lunches and leave Chincoteague on these two boats on a Saturday about noon and go to Franklin City, and this excursion train would take 'em (through Stockton, Girdletree, Berlin and up the line) to Philadelphia. They would change trains and go to Atlantic City and get to Atlantic City about ten o'clock Sunday morning, and leave about four o'clock Sunday afternoon by train back to Philadelphia and...back to Franklin City.

The fortunes of Scott's Ocean Beach House changed for the worse before the nineteenth century drew to a close, a casualty of the founding of Ocean City. The new village resort became more accessible from the city *via* the rail line and bridge across the Sinepuxent Bay, which in 1874 connected directly to Ocean City. In 1875 the Atlantic Hotel, a grandiose structure for its time, was built in Ocean City, and the tourists flocked to it; thus, ending any serious competition between the two beach attractions. Some accounts have it that Scott's closed in 1894, but there are reliable reports that the hotel was still struggling on as late as 1913. One on-site report shortly thereafter describes a once-bustling spa fallen into decay—the only signs of life being a sow and nine little pigs rooting around the vacant grounds.

As the island settlements withered away in the early 1900s, some of the parcels of land were bought for vacation homes or by gunning clubs. By the time Assateague Island National Seashore was established in 1965, there were approximately fifty cottages on the island. The cottages have since been hauled away, a step in returning the island to its original, natural state. Several of the vacated gunning club structures still remain, awaiting a Park Service decision on their use, or another major coastal storm to determine their fate. Waterfowl gunning has been allowed to continue, however, with public duck blinds made available through the National Park Service on a first-come basis.

The railroad to Ocean City that hastened the end of Scott's Ocean Beach House is now also long-gone; the bridge demolished by the 1933 Hurricane and the railroad right-of-way from Berlin to Ocean City sold away.

The former site of the bridge may be noted on the mainland across from the Ocean City Inlet, next to "Stinky Beach," at the end of Route 707. More than a century ago the rail line had allowed passengers to board (or change from Ocean City) at the Berlin junction, reach Philadelphia for lunch, have time in the afternoon for shopping or business appointments, and return home in the evening of the same day. This compared favorably with the two-day round-trip to Baltimore by a combination of buggy, rail, and steamboat. No wonder the seaside felt stronger ties with coastal cities to the north and south. From the time of the Assateague Indians through several centuries of English settlement, the "Western Shore" was a foreign land, and for some it still is.

Bob Phillips (NPS: 1978)

If we ever saw a strange track, automobile or foot track, we'd follow it to see who the devil was on the island 'cause we knew they'd be friends of ours. 'Cause my history on the island (goes way back) when the Coast Guard Station was in operation and I can remember when we were building that shanty up by the Jones' salt works. The Coast

> Guard helped us with this old white horse and a horse cart to carry some of the lumber from where we brought it over on the boat to the high sand hill, and built it there. And my job as a kid was keepin' the mosquitoes off the Coast Guardsmen drivin' the horse. And I'd have a bush in each hand. One for him and one for me. And if I would stop for a minute, his blue denim shirt you couldn't tell it was blue hardly for the mosquitoes and flies.
>
> And he would have on a short-sleeve shirt and maybe once a minute he would take his hand and do that (swat) and the blood would just come. And they never bothered him. He didn't know what it was. He'd say, "Oh, I leave 'em alone. When they once fill up they won't bother you no more."

Until the 1933 Hurricane, which opened the permanent inlet on the south end of Ocean City, the beaches of Assateague and Ocean City were one continuous strand. Neither Assateague nor Ocean City were islands as thought of today. During this pre-1933 era, Ocean City had been as important for its commercial fishing industry as for tourism. An estimated half-dozen fish camps were located in the vicinity of the present knoll on Assateague Island, just below what is now the Ocean City Inlet's south jetty. Each camp represented a separate fish company, or "fish industry."

Many of the fishermen were itinerant workers, coming up for the fishing season from Virginia and North Carolina. With no inland harbors to access behind Ocean City, the fishermen had to launch their heavy clinker-built skiffs off the beach to tend the fish-pound nets. These were stationary, funnel-type traps set just offshore, with long anchoring poles that could be seen from the mainland. Clydesdale-type work horses were rigged to pull the skiffs back onto the beach, usually loaded to the gunnels with fish. Among the catch were often large sturgeon—now rare in these waters—which would be stripped of their roes for salting, icing, and shipping by rail to the city markets. Before a modern ice house was built in Ocean City, the ice used for preserving the fish and roe was cut from the frozen bays in winter and stored under insulating layers of straw. That may also say something about differences in climate temperature between then and now.

Then came the big blow, and the beginning of the modern era along the seaside. Various local and national newspapers reported that no storm like the 1933 Hurricane had visited the Maryland coastline within the memory of its oldest inhabitants. A staff correspondent of the *Sun*, who was a witness, reported: "Far out to sea the waters could be seen rearing their heads many feet high and rolling into the beach. They would break against the houses and sweep across the island to mingle with the bay. Every wave cut away a portion of the sand, and generally carried a number of piles, and still further weakened the already tottering support of the houses. Wreckage is strewn from one end of the beach to the other. Bureaus, bedsteads, tables, chairs and every kind of furniture could be seen floating around the water. Near Congress Hall a handsome piano was standing on end almost buried in the sand, and the other half reared in the air, the surf breaking against it at every wave."

The hurricane swept away the fish camps, destroyed many of the fish pounds, and changed the commercial fishing industry from then on. Large mobile fishing trawlers, harbored safely behind the new inlet, were free to drag their nets all over the ocean. The hurricane's effects would also change the face of development in Ocean City. Tourism burgeoned and commercial fishing was overtaken by the birth of a recreational and sport fishing industry centered in the safe havens behind the beach resort.

Sport fishing can be dated to the summer of 1934, when the brothers Paul and Jack Townsend, local businessmen, located schools of white marlin some twenty-one miles offshore at Jack's Pot—a shoal named after an old-time local mariner. However, the location is now designated on charts as the Jack Spot, or Jack's Pot, in the belief that the name was attributable to Jack Townsend. Over the next several years, sport fishermen would begin to catch marlin regularly around Jack's Pot, and Ocean City quickly referred to itself as the White Marlin Capital of the World.

Similar impacts from the 1933 Hurricane were also felt at the other end of the coastal bays, on the southern tip of Assateague and on Chincoteague Island. It spelled the very end

Island Settlements of the Past

of what had remained of the clustered settlements along the beach, and severely tested the resilience of that hardy breed of Teaguers who clung to Chincoteague Island. Yet, just one generation later, a last effort would be made to exploit the island with residential and commercial development. Two major projects were approved by the Worcester County Commissioners after World War II: one proposed by Atlantic Beach Estates Corporation along four miles of North Beach, and a more ambitious project planned by the Ocean Beach Corporation for much of the rest of the Maryland portion of the island. Real estate salesmen with prospective buyers in tow filled the small ferry that ran "on call" between South Point and Assateague Island—piloted by the likable "Pot Pie" Purnell. Street signs began to sprout from the sand, promising busy roadways, motels, and fast-food emporia. Within a short period of time, the Ocean Beach Corporation had sold nearly 6,000 lots, and electric lines were being run from mainland to beach.

Don Bowden, Sr. (NPS: 1978)

About thirty years ago, I guess, a concern headed by a man by the name of Ackerman went over to Assateague and somebody invented an idea of mixing tar with beach sand, and he made a road several miles down and sold several million dollars worth of lots where the federal government has since bought most of the land. Oh, he had great plans. He had streets laid off. He had about ten miles of Main Street and then he had streets running each way from Main Street. And he had street signs and this hardtop surface was there for about ten or twelve miles down the beach. You had to get on the island then by McCabe's ferry. You would go down to South Point and get on this ferry and it would carry you across...and when you wanted to come back, they had a flag on a pole and they would raise the flag, and the people over at South Point (Jack "Pot Pie" Purnell) would keep an eye out and bring 'em back.

The developers' dreams quickly faded during a three-day blow in March 1962. One of the worst nor'easters of the century caused coastal damage almost as great as the '33 Hurricane, revealing the folly of further development. The prospective street signs were scattered as far ashore as high ground on the mainland. Once more, a bet on permanently settling the island would have been misplaced.

By-gone Life on the Barrier Island

Historic island settlements have largely vanished. Coastal storms have taken their toll. Vacation cottages built during the 1900s have been removed. Several vacated gunning shanties remain. A reconstructed and relocated Coast Guard station now stands at Tom's Cove. Assateague Island has returned to nature.

Crew of the Assateague Beach Life-Saving Station stands in front of the boathouse with rescue boat and cannon, circa 1905.

Norman Jones collection: courtesy of National Park Service

Popes Island Life-Saving Station was lost to fire in 1970.

Assateague Village did not survive the 1933 Hurricane. Pictured is one of the last surviving cottages.

Photos circa 1930: courtesy of National Park Service

1992 Nor'easter Finishes McCabe House

Constructed in the 1930s, McCabe House became the most palatial retreat on Assateague Island. Tom McCabe was a local boy who made good: corporate CEO, Chairman of the Federal Reserve Board, friend of U.S. Presidents, and lover of the coastal bays.

The National Park Service assumed ownership of McCabe House and used its quarters for some of the ranger staff, even as the ocean crept ever closer to its foundation. The January '92 nor'easter damaged the house irreparably—the remains were broken into pieces and carted off the island. The site, once a beacon to fishermen at sea, is well-remembered by all those who plied the nearby waters.

Photos 1992, courtesy of National Park Service

VII

Each tells its own familiar story,
the kingfisher perched on a post by the dock
erupts in brief bursts of comic joy,
while the restless willet regales on end
like the wandering tattler, ever full of it.

Seaside Legends, Yarns, & Other Tales

Rainbow at night, sailors' delight,
Rainbow in the morning, sailors take warning.

Ring around the moon,
Bad weather soon.

Rain before seven,
Clear before eleven.

When sheep collect and huddle,
Tomorrow there'll be a puddle.

A sunshine shower won't last an hour.

Folkloric weather prophesies may have been no more or less accurate than current weather forecasts delivered by meteorologists. Yet, at the very least, the old sayings conveyed a better sense of the historic dependence of local fishermen and farmers on Mother Nature.

Over time, the traditions of oral history have been interwoven with local pastimes: gathering around a kerosene heater in one of the gunning shanties, trading stories about red-letter days of the past; and fishing tales swapped much the same way, at dockside;

men-talk mostly, relaxed and fraternal. Yet, the ladies have held their own, too, sometimes in surprising language, at church socials and at card clubs that hold records in longevity. One such card club recently closed down, after spanning most of the twentieth century, with several of its members hanging on to the bitter end: sweet old ladies, dressed in finery, telling stories that could make a young maiden blush.

The oral history of Maryland's coastal bays still plays out, though at a faltering frequency, at local Mom and Pop stores and, in the evening, when native families get together and swap tales during the social hour. Much of the talk, like elsewhere on the Eastern Shore, is currently about local political shenanigans, duck hunting, and getting the pickup truck repaired. This oral tradition fills in the gaps in recorded history about infamous pirates finding refuge in the shallow sloughs behind Assateague Island, of their still-buried loot, of memorable shipwrecks and prominent bootleggers. In a more respectable vein are stories like that of the country's first great naval hero, Stephen Decatur.

At the local hardware store in Berlin, it's still possible to swap small talk while warming one's hands over a cast-iron wood stove. The smoky aroma wends through the place, as the chill of a wintry morning dissolves. Town folks come and go. After all, where else to catch up on the news or find such unfashionable items as a good wire clam basket or a Case penknife? Sorry, strike the clam basket. It is no longer in stock. Not made anymore, a dreadful portent of the future. Such establishments are barely holding on in the face of competition from a nearby Wal-Mart and Home Depot. When the hammer falls, the initial loss will be friendly, one-on-one service. Over time, the greater loss may be the closing down of another conduit of the oral tradition.

Such conversations may drift into dialect, when an older generation of rural folks get together, reminiscing about a county of dirt roads, colder winters, and no electricity. Although, as elsewhere, the old manner of speech is dying out. Not too long ago an eavesdropper might have thought that "it was fittin'" meant the speaker had been trying on some new clothes rather than complimenting a covered-dish supper at one of the local churches, or buying a "hoos" referred to a length of garden hose, and not a home dwelling. A "quar" fellow was not necessarily gay, just odd. The accents are several centuries distanced from the language transported to the Eastern Shore from the shires of England and softened with a faint Southern accent. Still, a hint of the past is still there, if one listens closely. And listening to the talk is as much of this travel, past and present, as hearing the chatter and calls of water birds in the marsh on a "ca'm" day.

One of the accomplished raconteurs is a local attorney whose family has been rooted in the seaside since the first wave of settlers, and whose repertoire borrows from this heritage. His tales take on an added glow and variation as the evening wears on, as in this condensed recounting of "Captain Eddie Meets the Witch of Assateague," a version of accounts about a young Dutch woman, Matilda van Eck :

Edward Hammond, Jr. (TP: 2002)

Around 1700, Edward Hammond (ancestor of the narrator), captain in the local militia, affectionately known as "Captain Eddie," enjoyed a colorful reputation in Somerset, now Worcester County. He was, by all accounts, a rake and a scoundrel, albeit for a time a vestryman at All Hallows, Church of England, in Snow Hill. He lived in Queponco, which is the large plantation area west of Newark, which he had stolen fair and square from the Indians earlier in the seventeenth century.

This wealthy gentleman had, however, one significant downfall: he was a skirt chaser. In his will, he left significant land and sums of money to the children of a lady friend, Hester Dioll—any dolt can figure out why—and was actually sued once by a man named Enoch Griffith, who prayed the Court to place Captain Hammond under a Peace Bond to keep him away from his wife, Jane Griffith. The handwritten testimony, which can be found to this day in the court records in Princess Anne, is quite colorful.

As a result of his proclivities, our hero was, alas, finally removed from the vestry, but at the time of his meeting with the Witch of Assateague he was a vestryman in good standing. It seems that the vestrymen—and they were, of course, all men—had gotten word that a Dutch woman had arrived on Assateague from Whore Kill, a Dutch settlement now known as Lewes, Delaware. It was named for a creek nearby, the word "kill" being Dutch for creek, and was so named because the Dutch sailors apparently got the Spanish disease from the local ladies upon landing. At any rate, this lady was apparently performing black magic on the island.

The vestrymen were outraged that such pagan activity should take place within their parish and decided to go to the island, seize her, and burn her at the stake. Captain Hammond, however, realizing that this could be a tragic waste of woman flesh, convinced the vestry to go to Assateague, apprehend her, and bring her into the Sanctuary at All Hallows Church—at which time, if she were in fact a witch, "the Lord would strike her dead." It's presumed that Captain Hammond was not so religious as to actually believe that such a thing would happen, but he figured it might be a good opportunity to broaden his field of play. The vestry left from what is now Public Landing and rowed to Assateague, where after some searching they spied the witch walking along the beach in a gray and black robe. They commenced to pursue her but as they drew close, a flock of geese flew over her and our Witch of Assateague flew off with the geese, but not before she cursed the island and said that in the 33rd year of every century there would be a terrible storm.

> **I'm not sure what might have happened in 1733 or 1833, but in 1933 Ocean City and Assateague Island suffered their worst storm ever.**

It's quite possible that a portion of this story is true (vestry records supposedly refer to the incident). That Matilda van Eck reportedly slipped away from the vestrymen along with a flight of geese may have been an excuse for the vestry's ineptitude in the hunt, or some clever stratagem of Captain Eddie. That witchery was ascribed to the Dutch woman was normal for the times; the accused were usually from enemy countries or out-of-favor religious sects, and in this case the English and Dutch were periodically at war on the high seas, as well as squabbling over proper location of the Maryland-Delaware state line.

Closer to historical fact are the documented records of the coastal bays having been a haven for some of the most nefarious pirates of colonial times. Since the first settlers arrived, the desolate beaches of Assateague Island and the shallow, concealed coves of the bays provided an ideal hiding place for the pirates' swift, shallow-drafted corsairs. The tales of the brigands who plied these waters in the 1700s and 1800s have always gripped the imagination—to the extent that even into the beginning of the past century many of the remaining residents were afraid to walk about Assateague Island at night.

Most infamous among these early pirates were Calico Jack and Edward Teach. The latter became better known as Blackbeard, sea captain from a reputable English family who turned outlaw. A story goes that one of Blackbeard's fourteen wives was stashed away on Assateague Island. Blackbeard himself was eventually captured and killed near Ocracoke, North Carolina. Whatever happened to the many wives is left untold.

Charles Wilson, a South Carolinian sea captain and privateer who also crossed the line into piracy, was to become even more appealing to local treasure hunters. During the 1950s, a widely circulated story had surfaced about Wilson leaving a treasure-filled chest buried on Assateague. As the story goes, Wilson was eventually caught, tried by the British Admiralty Court, and hanged in London in 1750. However, before his hanging, Wilson wrote a letter to his brother about a fabulous treasure he had hidden on the island. The letter, which was reportedly discovered some 200 years later in an old trunk in Germany, gave the treasure's location and described the contents as a fortune in gold, silver, and precious gems:

"To my brother George, there are three creeks lying 100 paces or more north of the second inlet above Chincoteague Island, Virginia, which is at the southward end of the Peninsula. At the head of the third creek to northward is a bluff facing the Atlantic Ocean with cedar trees growing on it each about 1 1/3 yards apart. Between the trees I buried in ten ironbound chests bars of silver, gold, diamonds and jewels to the sum of 200,000 pounds sterling. Go to 'Woody Knoll' secretly and remove the treasure.

Signed

Charles Wilson"

Not surprisingly, Assateague has changed so much over the years that the described site has yet to be found. The loaded trunks that supposedly rested near twin red cedars, possibly on a sandy rise somewhere near Green Run, could have been where an inlet later cut through; such have been the shifting of sands. Or the cache may be resting at the bottom of the ocean, just beyond the waves breaking in the surf, as a result of rising sea levels and the westward rolling over of the island. The whole story may also be apocryphal. The missing letter is still missing, except in the fanciful mind of the treasure hunter.

A ditty of local folklore, reputedly matched to the rhythm of a watchful magpie's chatter (though perhaps more appropriately pitched to the shrill, telltale cry along the marsh of the mating willet, a member of the tattler family of shorebirds), captures the spirit of dashed hopes of treasure hunters searching for the buried pots of gold left over from shipwrecked galleons along the Delmarva coastline in days of yore:

"See one (magpie),

That's for sorrow," goes the magpie (or willet).

See two,

That's for mirth,

See three,

That's a wedding,

See four,

That's a birth,

See five,

That's for silver,

See six,

That's for gold,

See seven,

That's for a secret, never to be told."

More Strange Happenings on Assateague
Nat Steelman (NPS: 1971)

My father in his younger days was in the Life-Saving Service at Pope's Island on Assateague right at the Maryland-Virginia border, just in Virginia. Anyway, he was going down the beach one night to his key post. When he got ready to come back, he saw a small light along the hills and it come toward him and when it got right to him he said it got as big as a clothes basket. Scared the starch out of 'im, so to speak. Maybe modern man might say it was a jack-o-lantern or somethin'. So it happened a few nights after this, three head went down the beach near that same spot...it had been a wreck right there and a yawl boat—a double-ended row boat—was pulled up on the bank and the servicemen had turned 'er over and set a prop under one end, so it rains they could get under there in shelter.

So it was a stormy night and two of 'em decided to go to the surf to see if they could see anything, and one of 'em set under the boat...while dey was gone dis boat shook and shook. Dere weren't any wind and this fella got scared. He come out o' dere. He went and told the other two, so dey poked fun at him. When dey come back, de boat shook so

bad dey all run....Now right at the same spot a Mister Wise Dunn, long dead now, was supposed to have found enough money that he went on the mainland and bought a farm.

If the shallow and secluded waters of the coastal bays provided shelter for pirates, these same conditions were also a defense against British warships in colonial times. They provided a haven for the Stephen Decatur family during the British siege of Philadelphia in 1778-79. A merchant shipper, Stephen Decatur's father was familiar with the local ports and brought his pregnant wife through the Sinepuxent Inlet, across Newport Bay, and up the narrow reaches of Trappe Creek, where humble lodgings were secured for the birth in 1779 of this young country's first great naval hero. Though the newborn Stephen was soon transported back to Philadelphia, after very few diaper changes, his name abounds locally on school buildings, parks, and streets and highways.

At age 25, following his daring missions at sea, Stephen Decatur became the youngest officer to ever captain a ship in the young American Navy. On the night of February 16, 1804, Lieutenant Decatur, with a crew of volunteers, had slipped into the harbor at Tripoli on the pirate-infested Barbary Coast in the Mediterranean Sea. After furious hand-to-hand combat, Decatur burned the American frigate *Philadelphia* that had been previously captured by the pirates. British Admiral Lord Nelson declared this "the most bold and daring act of the age." Later, during the War of 1812, Decatur captained the frigate *United States* into battle with the powerful British warship *Macedonian* and brought her in to port as a prize.

When Decatur died in 1822 at the age of 41 from a dueling wound, his national popularity was such that his funeral was attended by an estimated 10,000 people—80 percent of the population of Washington, D.C. Today, Stephen Decatur may be best remembered for his patriotic words delivered as a toast at a dinner party in Norfolk in 1815: "Our country! In her intercourse with foreign nations may she always be in the right; but our country right or wrong!" Sounds familiar.

As a historical footnote, the Decatur birthplace, a one-story, cypress-framed building, stood on the edge of Berlin until the 1920s, when it was bought by Sears & Roebuck as a promotion for its "long-lasting" home-building materials. Sears shipped the dwelling around the country on a flat-bed railroad car, after which, according to local versions of the story, the structure was broken into pieces and sold at auction. So much for historic preservation in those days. Recently, however, there has been some talk by the Town of Berlin about replicating the Decatur home and recapturing this piece of local heritage.

While the secluded waters of the coastal bays may have meant security to the Decatur family, the ocean shoals on the opposite of islands spelled danger to coastal mariners.

When boats came aground in the stormy surfs of Assateague, it was frequently a race between sharp-eyed islanders and insurance agents to see who would lay claim to the prize cargo. One famous incident occurred when the ship *Lively*, bound from Amsterdam to New York and laden with over 7,000 gallons of gin, wrecked on the shores of Assateague in 1796. In the free-for-all that followed, John Fassitt, who lived just across the Sinepuxent Bay at the still-extant Henry's Grove, laid first claim to the gin as salvage. Though challenged in court by the cargo's owner, the case dragged on for some years until all the gin had disappeared. Fassitt himself had died after carefully dispensing, according to the embellishments of local legend, the many hogsheads (barrels) of evidence.

Fassitt may have turned over in his grave upon divining that the "Drys" of Worcester County had recovered their voice by the early 1900s and launched a tumultuous assault against demon rum. Demonstrators marched down the Main Streets of the local villages, the youth of the county oddly joined with their elders in shouting:

> Whiskey's going, whiskey's going, whiskey's gone;
>
> Vote on! Vote on!
>
> Everybody, everybody,
>
> Join the whole Protection Party!

United across the country, the "Drys" pressured Congress to pass the Prohibition Amendment in 1919, followed by enforcement measures of the Volstead Act in 1920.

Rejoicing could be heard throughout most of the Protestant community, although a somewhat laissez-faire attitude was reported among Episcopalians. In any case, the more subdued "Wets" quietly kept their spirits up and flowing during a parched decade that would end with the repeal of Prohibition in 1933. Liquor closets remained well stocked, as contraband supplies rolled onto the county beaches with the persistence of ocean waves. The vacant stretches of Assateague Island were ideal for the rum-runners to land their cargoes ashore, much as pirates had used the barrier islands in past centuries.

Several highly publicized arrests of rum-runners would make good reading in the local newspapers. In 1930, twenty-nine Worcester County men, many of them in high standing around Ocean City and Berlin, were nabbed by the Coast Guard, along with the seizure of $250,000, about four miles below Ocean City. Newspaper photos show several local, thirsty-looking businessmen standing with the Coast Guardsmen. A photo caption noted, "No need for the ardent Drys to worry about this liquor as it has all but disappeared into that great unknown from which there is no return."

Bootlegging During Prohibition
Kendall Jarvis (THM: 2001)

James Richard Phillips, the local canner, had a cabin approximately a mile north of the old North Beach Lifesaving Station. We went down for a hunting trip. We had a fair shooting morning but ran out of whiskey, so we decided to come to Berlin to get some. I had an old '29 Ford Roadster as I recall, and I started up the beach. We saw what we called a fish pound boat, a clinker-built boat. I came on the beach and started unloading bundles. Bundles that later turned out to be boot-leg whiskey. Good Whiskey. Golden Wedding and various other brands. Not being greedy, of course, but being curious, so we tried and got some.

There were trucks hauling it from the beach. The trucks were hauling this stuff from Assateague to a boat on a shoal on the west side of the beach, then they were carrying it across the bay in another boat and landed at what we call Ayers Point. And there they were loading it into trucks marked John Wanamaker.

They (Coast Guard) caught so many who were involved, they were jailed, put on their honor, whatever, in Ocean City. Later they were put the same way up in Denton...it got rather involved and involved a lot of prominent people and it kind of blew away in time.

Sally Bunting (THM: 2001)

We were living at the hotel (in Ocean City) and this group of men came and rented several rooms. It was the depression and nobody had any money, everybody was dirt poor. Well, we had a pay phone, one man sat by the pay phone all the time and there were different ones coming in and out. Nobody mentioned the word rum-running, but half of the county were involved. The farmers, they were using mules, even my husband (Josh Bunting), who had been about thirteen or fourteen years old, was running messages for them. Of course, he was not going to tell anybody, his two brothers were in the Coast Guard and when they arrested the bootleggers and their helpers they grabbed Josh, too.

Well, anyway, when the news came out from the telephone booth that they had been caught, they were unloading the ship...they said to my mother, "What is the quickest way to get to a railroad station, we want to get to Wilmington, Delaware, in a hurry." She said, "Well, you'd have to wait I guess for the noon train." And they said, "Well, is there any way we..." and she said, "Well, maybe Mr. Gunby would take you, the taxi driver." So they hauled off, all of them weren't on the beach. Mr. Gunby took them to Wilmington and put them on the train, and they left their clothes and everything.

> One of them called my father, they had them in the Snow Hill jail, the ones they caught on the beach...so he went down to the jail and the man put his hand through the bar to shake hands with him and when he did he put a great big diamond ring in his hand and he said, "Would you keep this for me?"...When they had the trial Daddy had to get up on the stand and they made this one man stand up who was the leader, he found out later, and said (to Daddy), "Do you recognize this man?" And Daddy said, to be honest there were so many of them, he didn't know who was who and he said, "No, I don't think I ever saw him in my life." That man got off. When Daddy walked out of the court house, this man and another man with him, walked out to him and said, "Mr. Dennis, I want to thank you." Daddy said, "I'll be honest, I don't remember seeing you in my life." So he handed Daddy a card and said, "If you ever come to New York, look me up and don't forget it...." So a couple of years later Daddy went to New York to visit his sister who lived right in the city and he said he got bored to death hanging around her apartment, so he pulled out this card....He got in the cab and handed the card and asked if (the cabby) knew where this is. He said, "Sure!" Daddy said he went in the worst looking, run-down old bar and he said to the bartender, "Do you know this man?" He said, "Yeah, just a minute." So he made a phone call and in a couple of minutes another fellow came and said, "Come upstairs." Daddy said he went up and it was one of the most beautiful apartments he had ever seen. "He was the kingpin and he wined me and dined me in New York."

Lucrative treasure hunts along the surf bank have been further victimized by the seaworthiness of modern vessels with high-tech navigational equipment, minimizing the likelihood of shipwreck or salvageable ballast winding up on the beach. The Park Service also keeps a close eye on the flotsam and jetsam, rightfully claiming anything of value. However, beach-walking remains an enjoyable pastime, with the occasional surprise of an unusual seashell or the temporary uncovering of the skeleton of an old shipwreck after a nor'easter.

Then there is always the sheer contentment of just wandering along the edge of the sea, on a beach that is ever changing and yet remains much the same. The cries of gulls carry through the salt air and the lulling churn of waves, folding over in the surf, drifts across the island, mixed with visions of pirates, bootleggers, shipwrecks, and fortunes in treasure just beneath the sand.

CONTEMPORARY VIEWS—IN COLOR— OF A FRAGILE HERITAGE

Costal Bays by Aerial Photographer Andrew Serrell

"Serenity" Nature Scenes by Professional Photographer Mike Gatty

Painting & Photo by Patrick Henry
www.henryfinearts.com

Bridges of Change

Lifestyles changed rapidly after World War II. The automobile made families more mobile and summer vacations at the shore became the mode. One deterrent was getting across the Chesapeake Bay other than by ferry. When the Bay Bridge opened in 1952, centuries of isolation of Maryland's seaside soon ended. The Route 90 Bridge, above, spans the Assawoman Bay between the late 20th century mainland community of Ocean Pines and the recent high-rise section of North Ocean City. The era of a low-key resort village by the sea had come to an end.

Sinepuxent, from Ocean City Inlet to South Point

The erosion and movement of Assateague Island south of Ocean City Inlet is apparent at the top-right. The beach has been nearly stripped of vegetation. The narrow strand of beach bellows westward, toward the mainland. In time, the two bodies are likely to merge.

Since this photo was taken in the 1980s, new residential construction and golf course developments have crept down the mainland shoreline, replacing farmlands. The southern-most tip of land, South Point, is surrounded by three of the five coastal bays: Sinepuxent Bay to the east, Newport bay to the west, and Chincoteague Bay at the south tip.

Ayers & Trappe Creeks, Tributary to Newport Bay

A thought-provoking water trail, Ayers Creek joins Trappe Creek and together they open into Newport Bay. Known in colonial times as Assateague Creek, the tributary marks a division between the expanding urbanization of Sinepuxent and the natural tidewater vistas of the lower coastal bays. Paddlers may enter the creek at the bridge, as shown, on Rt. 376 as it nears Rt. 611.

Lower Coastal Bays

Below Berlin, a still largely-rural Worcester County comes into view. The backcountry along the Chincoteague Bay still moves at a slower pace. Here, the tidal waters are the cleanest on the seaside, or in the state. Expanses of farmland—some 1,000 acres or more—now include large tracts placed under conservation easements in perpetuity. Pine and mixed-hardwood forests account for a large portion of most properties. Assateague Island frames the background. Boaters are spare: mostly commercial crabbers in summer, clammers in winter, and duck hinters in season—plus a few locals, enjoying an outing on the water.

"Serenity"

Painting (top) and Photo (bottom) by Patrick Henry

VIII

At home in the guts and sloughs
when the coastal bays were young,
the wily black duck is still the sign
that matters most among old proggers,
who see it in decline.

End of an Era, Two Word Wars, And One Great Progger

St. Paul's Episcopal Church Cemetery Gravestone Marking

CAREY

Ethan Allen   Addie B. Henry
1874-1953   1872-1973

The bodies lie side by side, flanked by their relatives and friends, "first families" of the seaside, who were born in the era surrounding the Civil War and lived on through much of the twentieth century.

The number may be counted on one hand, as of this writing, of centenarians residing along the coastal bays, whose lives began in that distant nineteenth century and then stretched forward across two more century marks. What these and other venerable senior citizens have beheld over these past 100 years has been the incredible change from a colonial Anglo-American horse-and-buggy culture to the wonders of cyberspace.

In the first half of these senior citizens' lives, little had changed since the first English merchant-planters staked out their expansive farmlands, and village settlements began to flourish along the waterways and down the old Philadelphia Post Road, now Rt. 113. It was a past that existed on borrowed time, and omens of an unsettling future mingled with the traditional lifestyle. During both world wars, what might now be termed German "terrorist" attacks on merchant shipping lanes just off Assateague Island panicked the seaside, much the same way as the terrorist attacks of September 11, 2001 affected the nation. The Great Depression of the 1930s would linger here for ten long years, only to subside when economic prosperity returned as a benefit of World War II. Yet, through it all, the quality of seaside life, complacent as it seems to have been, was being gradually brought up to date by improved health care, electricity, and the gasoline engine.

A century after the British blockades ended along the Atlantic Coast, following the War of 1812, foreign threats to the American homeland began all over again. In World War I, German U-boats feasted on American and Allied merchant vessels. The most notorious German submarine, U-151, was credited with sinking twenty-three ships along the Atlantic Coast, several in the vicinity of Assateague Island, on one three-month outing alone. On the same cruise, U-151 laid mines and cut trans-Atlantic cables off New York City. Several of the relics from U-151 and subsequent enemy submarines still lie at the bottom of the sea off the Maryland and Delaware coasts—now affording some recompense in the way of good fishing spots.

The Taylor House Museum in Berlin, a fine repository of local heritage, and well worth a visit, displays in one of its many exhibit panels the following footnote on World War I:

"Germans Near Here! A startling message found on Ocean City Beach. 2 miles north of Ocean City a glass bottle enclosing a piece of greasy cardboard bearing the following words written in lead pencil. 'I am a prisoner on a German gunboat. Overthrow of German Government plans. I think we are near New York. 10-15 submarines. I think I will be drowned tonight.' The signature was not legible and was found with several others and a few large onions and oranges and small wreckage apparently just washed up by the seas."

The U-boat harassment was repeated during World War II. In the period of January-June 1942 alone, some 360 merchant ships were sunk along the Eastern Seaboard. German Admiral Doenitz boasted at the time, "Our submarines are operating close inshore along the coast of the United States of America, so that bathers and sometimes entire coastal cities are witnesses to the drama of war, whose visual climaxes are constituted by the red glorioles (halos) of blazing tankers." Doenitz's comment was certainly true locally, for on at least two occasions American tankers were blown up within sight of Assateague Island, and the ships blazing in the night could be readily seen ashore.

So great was the menace of German submarines and the fear of an actual invasion that military defenses—chiefly, "pill-box" emplacements—were built beneath the Ocean City boardwalk, and military vehicles constantly patrolled the beaches of Assateague Island for landings of enemy scouts and saboteurs. A civilian militia was formed locally to support regular military forces, and the militia was equipped with like-new Army Springfield Cal. 4570 rifles, relics from the Spanish-American War that had been stored by the government in their original packing cases for a half-century. Volunteers were also enlisted as plane-spotters, with concern that an enemy squadron or reconnaissance plane might pass over on the way to a Washington or Baltimore target. Any local schoolboy could instantly tell the difference between a bent-wing German Stuka dive-bomber and a Messerschmitt fighter plane.

If this response to foreign attack now seems overblown, the reality of war seemed close at hand. Military planes droned overhead, and civilians were required to dampen car headlights and pull their shades at night. Military convoys clogged the local roads. Merchant ships were being torpedoed just offshore. The bodies of American seaman were washing onto Assateague Island. This was "high alert" time.

Oral Histories taken in 1995 by the Berlin Heritage Foundation (Taylor House Museum) to celebrate the 50th anniversary of the end of World War II:

Bob Wimbrow

There was a drastic change after December 7, 1941...There was a lot of patriotism at that point in time that we haven't had since, I don't think. Everybody backed the war effort. Not many people dodged the draft...even down in the rural areas where farmers were deferred, it was easy getting a deferment, (but) a lot of these guys you're reading about went voluntarily...Of course, the very first thing that I remember associated with World War II was Ethiopia. It was in the *Weekly Reader* every week. The Italian Army was flexing their muscles in Ethiopia. Getting practice was what they were doing. Then, of course, the next thing was Spain. Then the Germans were in Spain...So, you know, you could see it coming.

James Edward "Snooks" Lynch

I went into the service after...I turned 18. We went to the doctor's office—now it's the fire house, the old fire house back of City Hall (Berlin). That's where the first examination was that you went to. If you passed there, you then went to Baltimore for your physical. You got two physicals. If you got turned down there, that was it. I remember old Dr. Law, he would come in the soda fountain. There was a place where the counter went in a little ways and he always sat there. He was so funny, he'd say, "Lynchy, you want to go into the service?" I said yeah, you know, there was nothing to

do around here. And I often wondered since, if I said no—well, he was our family doctor: he "born me"—and I often wondered if he would see that I got turned down, if I said no.

John T. Bruehl

I was teaching shop (in Berlin)...and this was probably in 1940. We had an organizational meeting (Minutemen home militia). We had all kinds of firearms, from old firearms to muskets and all kinds of shotguns. We had to furnish your own arms, but they gave us some after we got started. They sent about two dozen 45-70s, originally made just a year or two after the Civil War, with ammunition from 1898. The uniform was Sears and Roebucks's blue jeans, blue shirt, and a blue kind of winter jacket...I just gave mine away around Christmas time. I had that thing that long. We also had fatigues...with leggings and all. Our helmets for summer were these pith helmets and in the winter time we had some kind of overseas cap. We had arm bands. If you didn't have your arm band on you'd be shot for a spy. That was our identification, Minutemen arm band.

You would have to listen for any planes, and also if you saw them there was a phone...and you'd call in certain numbers and you had to tell them if it was flying east, west, north or south and if it was flying high or low, and had to tell what kind of plane it was...Oh yeah, I had a beat. I had Powellton Avenue and Vine Street. At the telescope house, Mr. Hammond always had a light on; never could keep him from having that light on. Some of the folks said it might be best to have one light on so it didn't look like it was prepared for a blackout.

Coming back to these airplanes flying over...Hitler flew over here, and he looked down here and he saw these chicken houses lit up, tapped the old pilot and said we better turn back, they've got too many barracks down there.

Powell Esham

During the war I was too young for the first war and too old for the second war. I had the milk business and I had to have help to work for me. I had to stay home and work with them because they didn't know what to do and my wife drove the milk truck for two years. Then I had trouble, they didn't want me to have gasoline and we had to buy a horse and milk wagon to deliver milk in. Well, I'll tell you, I was surprised: I was such a big farmer in the dairy business that I eventually got stamps to get all the gasoline I wanted. I never had to wait for gasoline, but you had to get permission to get tires and stuff like that.

I asked the draft board why they didn't let me have the boys off the farms that knew how to work instead of letting me have the town boys. They told me that if I didn't want them somebody else would get them, so I just had to put up with them...On the road across from Stephen Decatur School was Harrison's Farm and the prisoner of war camp was there, German prisoners. You could get a permit and be responsible for them and get them to work for you...to kill sows for people and stuff like that. They could do anything, all you had to do was tell them what to do and they were smart, they could do anything. It was good help.

Bill Neville

One thing that woke us up to the reality of a war going on, Ray Coates and I used to go into Mr. Powell Esham's dairy field...which was somewhere around where Atlantic General (Hospital) is now. There wasn't any 113 by-pass through there then. Anyhow, (Powell Esham) used to let us go out in the back of the pastures and hit baseballs and we did that day after day to try to improve our ability as fielders and so forth. One day we heard this plane go overhead and then we could see the plane go down. It crashed.....We took off running and tried to get to the area, but by then they had it blocked off so we couldn't see the wreck. I think it was a two-engine Army Air Force bomber.

Matilda T. Burbage

...As long as he was overseas (husband Bill Burbage), I came back and helped my mother in the Eastern Shore Hotel, which she ran...I made all the blackout curtains. We had to have blackout curtains on every window because we were right on the ocean and of course the German ships were all out here, and the German submarines, and they did come in. They came in Chincoteague and bought Salisbury Bread. And they found the theater tickets on the German prisoners where they'd been to movies in Chincoteague. There was a boat off here and a German submarine came and surfaced and shot the men after they got in the lifeboat to come ashore. And the men were brought ashore in this boat and packed in a railroad car of ice. That's how they shipped the bodies away. I think there were about thirteen of them.

Dr. Frank Townsend

I believe it was Good Friday. I've forgotten what year now, but a ship was torpedoed off Ocean City, and the German submarines machine gunned the people in the boats. And they (Coast Guard) brought those people in and they unloaded them down at the ice plant and then drove them to Norfolk for distribution and burial. American sailors. Roland Farlow's father was out in the ocean at that time and they (Coast Guard) were asking him what his location was—they were talking back and forth with the station here. And (Roland) said, "I ain't gonna give you my location, Cap. Them Heinies are still all around out here and I'm scared." So he never told them where he was.

Along with the impact of two world wars on the first half of the twentieth century, a return to the year 1901 is marked by yet another milestone. On the far shores of the Atlantic Ocean, Queen Victoria died at age eighty-two. The Victorian Age, seemingly imbedded forever in this English-settled colony, would soon falter, though not without leaving behind a stereotyped picture of Victorian-style homes and village streets, a certain civilized politeness among its people, a way of dress, the care of the small farmer for his land, and an output of art and local craft that often bears the nineteenth century Victorian "look."

As one old-timer used to put it in a recurrent fit of nostalgia, "We have seen the best of times, m'boy, the best of times." And he may have been right. The natives whose lives were rooted in this immediate post-Victorian age are still looked back on with some awe. "He (or she) was the last of a generation," is the murmur that goes through the gathering at funerals for the dwindling number of these venerated souls.

Of all the memorable characters who lived along the coastal bays in this special time, none more fully embodied its spirit than Ethan Allen "Neath" Carey and his wife, Addie Byrd Henry Carey. Neath was a direct descendant of Capt. William Fassitt, the original grantee of Mayfields, the Careys' idyllic Sinepuxent Bayside farm dating to the seventeenth century. Addie Byrd was a descendent of the grantees of nearby Genezar, the earliest plantation in Sinepuxent Neck. She was the last surviving owner of a vast tract of waterfront property, including Genezar, that was acquired by Salisbury realtor Franklyn Woodcock on the eve of World War II. This marriage between the first families of Sinepuxent Neck continued a tradition. That the couple had no children was also becoming typical among a number of these founding families.

The Carey's graceful 200-year old plantation home faced out towards the bay. Like most other bayside homes of that age, it was built cautiously on the rise of fast land, well away from the water's edge. The enclosed sun porch facing southeast, unusually bright and generous with glass for the era, held a commanding view of the bay. Shelves were placed high against the glass and held every type and color of old bottle and glass buoy that had washed up on the beach over a lifetime. Neath collected them from Assateague Island for the better part of eighty years. He loved their look and feel, though thought them otherwise worthless. Today many of them, as collectibles, would be worth hundreds of dollars or more apiece.

The view from the sun porch carried through low pines, across the marsh, and along a narrow catwalk toward the boathouse. Here was Neath's other home, well-weathered, dedicated to the pleasures of the bay and ornamented inside and out with various creatures nailed like scalps to the cedar-sided walls. This was another time, not unlike the days of a James Audubon, when people were few and the varieties of wildlife were many. A bird skin, a muskrat or an otter pelt, or the jaws of a large shark hung up to dry did not seem like a strain on the natural resources. That a few shorebirds were shot for the kitchen seemed to matter little either. And Neath was a crack shot with his side-by-side, Damascus-steel-barreled Greener 12-gauge shotgun. Even when seasons were closed, Federal and State game laws did not reach out to country folk along the seaside.

Neath was a man's man, and at the same time a charmer of the ladies and children—with the manners of an earthy country gentleman and that speech and garb that goes with the coastal bays. Well-known scribes, artists, sportsmen, and entrepreneurs, as well as friends and relatives, descended constantly on Mayfields to spend a day with the bays' quintessential character. Neath befriended them all with unassuming lore and humorous tales of tidewater life.

True to his ancestral seafaring genes, Neath was a powerful swimmer. Of medium height, he was thick through the chest and shoulders from a lifetime of swimming out through the surf, as a one-time surfman with the Life-Saving Service, and from tonging oysters and raking clams, hunting over marshes and slough for waterfowl and terrapin, and working his crop land. Neath moved agilely for a man habitually wearing cumbersome knee-boots—"gumboots"—everywhere but to church and to bed. The English still wear their Wellingtons, or "Wellies," though the footwear is no longer as popular here.

Neath was perhaps the most resourceful progger the coastal bays have ever known. Progger is a term that was once applied favorably to those who poked opportunistically about the coastal bays. The verb "prog"—hence the noun, "progger"—has been passed down from old English and describes the gathering of food and other essentials in the wild. Locally, the progger was held to be an experienced and clever sort of scavenger, with a knack for finding abandoned prizes washed up along the shore. It mattered little if such foraging came close to the limits of the law. Neath set the standard for those proggers who would come later, naming just a few who come to mind: Herb Harmon and Ebe Elliot; followed by Earl and Mac Simpson, Lynches (Bud and Eddie), the Purnell brothers; more Elliots, two generations of Mumfords, and Judge Dale Cathell in his younger, adventurous days. The things they have known about the bays are beyond scientific study.

A characteristic view of Neath Carey was aboard his Chincoteague Bay scow, the *Addie Byrd*. The scow is a classic coastal bays boat. Geography has been a determinant again. Flat-bottomed, the scow is at home in the shallow coastal bays. The bow presents a wide, curving surface to short, choppy waves—not pointed like a fancy motor boat—and the boat can be run up onto the marsh and easily unloaded of gear and crew. The *Addie Byrd* was powered by a one-cylinder Palmer engine, famous at the time among watermen for its work-horse reliability. The "one-lunger's" resonant and unmistakable "put-put-put" sound echoing out over the bay on a still morning was its trademark. That "put-put" and the occasional shotgun blast from a hunter were about the only sounds to be heard on the bays for many years. An entire season could go by with no more than a half-dozen boats, pleasure and working craft with the *Addie Byrd* included, to be seen or heard. Day after day might go by without a soul in sight. And that was not so long ago.

"It's slick ca'm this morning, Addie, and getting on to high tide. I think we could use some fresh fish on hand." The voice came in a seaside pitch. As the *Addie Byrd* headed out into the windless morning, a soft vapor of low-lying fog would be just rising off the water, the faintest of cool air out of the east from the sea mingling with the warmer mainland temperature.

"It'll burn off shortly," Neath could have been thinking, as he would anchor up and bring out one of the long bamboo poles cut off a neighbor's stand and dried over the winter on a rack along the inside wall of the barn. No reel; just the line tied to the end and wound or unwound from around the pole as needed. The fishing hole was never too deep to interfere with lifting the tip of the pole skyward, and in one motion clearing the gunnel with fish flopping on the end of the line. Neither the finest split-bamboo fly rod nor top-of-the-line spinning gear could ever perform with greater satisfaction. In the winter, this progger might choose to search for air holes in the shallow bottom of a nearby cove and gig below for enough eels for supper. There was always food to be gathered from the bays, when one knew how.

Few of these old, solid-planked Chincoteague Bay scows are still in active use, although once in a while it's possible to spot a rotting relic that has been retired to a side yard, filled with some potting soil and planted with geraniums. The modern versions are fiberglass; it's not the same. A stern plate carrying the name *Addie Byrd* survives on cousin Ned Carey's fishing boat. A family tradition continues.

Of all the grand times that Neath Carey and his friends and relatives spent on the bay, none is more evocative than the seine-hauling parties. Pulling a net in those days, when the critters in the bay were in unimaginable abundance by today's standards, bore little resemblance to dragging a short length of net today to capture a few minnows and crabs for bait or to interpret the condition of the bays' resources.

With hundreds of feet of seine folded carefully on the broad stern seat of a rowboat, Neath would row out in an arc away from the point of marsh at the mouth of a favorite cove on an incoming tide, playing out the seine until it cut off all exit from the cove to open water in the bay. Long haul-lines attached to each end of the seine were given over to the helpers standing on the marsh, who would pull towards the head of the cove as if in a tug-of-war.

"Easy does it, little boy (or 'little girl,' no matter the age). Not too fast. Let the tide he'p you," came regularly from Neath. Then, as the net would begin to grow heavy with bay grass and the catch, swirls would ripple the water around the cork line and a few mullet (fatback) would squirt over the net to freedom. Finally, the pocket of the seine was pulled onto the marsh bank and, oh Lord, what a sight! Terrapin would be crawling out of the pocket in the net and eels slithering under the lead line and back into the cove; but mostly "a right smart" of fish and crabs would have been gathered up and pinned in the coils of grass. Finally came the truly fun part of sorting out the peelers and soft crabs and gathering the fish, pan-size and real jumbos, into any number of peach baskets. One haul alone could feed everyone in the party for days.

With luck, there was still time for another haul before the tide changed.

Oft' told Story by E. A. Carey (TP: c. 1947)

Shootin' yellowlegs, curlew and such were ag'in the law, but it's hard to stop something you've done all your life. And we're just talking about a few for the pot. I could go out anytime and stick up a few decoys along the edge of the marsh out on the point and sit down by a clump of kinks bushes, and pretty soon a bunch of yellowlegs or what-all would come by. The yellowlegs were easy to whistle in to you, you know, like this...WHEW, whew, whew. You could get your lips blistered if you were new at it, all that whistlin'.

Well, this one day Batty Mixon came by. He was the State Game Warden who covered most of these parts anywhere around here, and all the way over to the Chesapeake, so far as I know. Most gunners were scared of Batty because he was tough and he seemed to pop out of nowhere when you least wanted him around. But Batty and I always got along pretty good and he liked Addie's cooking. Anyway, this one day I'm in the boathouse getting ready to pick some birds I had shot that morning and I happened to look out through the porthole toward the catwalk, and here comes Batty ambling along over the marsh a little quicker than usual. Well, I had 'bout enough time to toss the birds in the bottom of a bucket and then fill the bucket up with a good mess of arsters I had just picked up along the shore.

After the usual pleasantries Batty says to me, "Did you hear any of that shootin' on the bay a little while ago?" So I wrinkled my forehead, kind of thinking, and says, "Reckon I did, but didn't pay much 'tention to it. A couple of proggers over by the sand island, I 'spect." Well, Batty kind of smiled 'cause he was no fool. He glanced around the boathouse, looking close, then shook his head. He wasn't going to push it. So then I says to him, "Batty, when you go back to the house, would you drop this bucket of arsters off with Addie. We haven't had a good arster stew for a time."

Well, I chuckled all the while Batty walked away down the catwalk, carrying the arsters and yellowlegs, and Addie and I laughed about that many a time later, though Addie never thought the trick on Batty was as funny as I did. And even though she filled him up on a couple of warm biscuits and my good ham, Addie always seemed to feel a little guilty. Anyways, I guess Batty was an accessory to the crime.

(Now looking back, it may have been that Batty Mixon remembered that morning differently. What if, when delivering the oysters to Addie Byrd, Batty had commented, "Neath said to drop off these oysters so you could fix a stew for supper." And Addie Byrd had exclaimed, "My land, why would he ever ask for another stew. We've had those oysters every night this week." It would never come to light if the warden left Mayfields with a knowing smirk on his face along with the salty taste of country ham in his mouth.)

Addie Byrd was a grand partner with an equally large following of admirers. When the action was out on the bay, she might stay behind to cook. It was rare that anyone ever left Mayfields hungry, if only just passing through. At the very least, a visitor would have to go away with a "scratch" biscuit made with the clabber left over from her butter-making and filled with the thin, salty slices of the Careys' home-smoked ham. Approaching age ninety, Addie Byrd was still picking and eating steamed crabs off yesterday's edition of *The Sun* spread out on the kitchen table of her last-owned dwelling in Berlin. That was the earthly side of Addie Byrd, the Victorian wife.

For the better part of a century she also filled St. Paul's Episcopal Church in Berlin with her spirituality, Bible teaching, and the hymn music she played on an old pump organ. Attending St. Paul's Church until her death at age 101, Addie Byrd was survived by few of her contemporaries—a notable exception being Mrs. James Richard Phillips, a matriarch of that prominent family, who passed away in 1997 at age 110. Occupying adjacent church pews for generations, Addie Byrd and Audrey ("Nana") Phillips established a remarkable standard in longevity.

Neath died in 1953, and in his mind he truly had seen the best of times. The shorebirds and black ducks were not like they used to be. Those fat curlew practically gone, the large sea trout harder to come by. These had been the halcyon days. Shortly after his death, Mayfields was sold, and before the decade was out vandals had burnt to the ground the fine old home. The property was subsequently developed as a western theme park and campground (Frontier Town). The facsimile saloon stands over the old smoke house and near the root cellar that once kept the apples and potatoes and enough fattening terrapins to provide "many a supper."

Addie Byrd lived on for another twenty years after Neath died, active in mind and spirit to the very end. She had lasted into the jet age and seen almost everything. What she thought she may have missed in a countrified life by age 90, she made up for by setting aside the steamed crabs for a few weeks and, during the turbulent sixties, taking an unaccompanied bus trip across the nation and back. It was a time of civil strife and student riots in the nation. But this she could look beyond. The country was doing all right, she reported on her return. People were nice all along the way.

Nearing age 100 she was visited in the nursing home by the Baltimore Orioles third baseman, Hall of Famer Brooks Robinson, who paid honor to the Orioles' most loyal fan.

A little over a year later, Addie Byrd Henry Carey was laid to rest beside her Neath in St. Paul's Episcopal Church cemetery in Berlin. There, as in nearby Buckingham Cemetery and Evergreen Cemetery, the mossy gravestones of the Fassitts, Henrys, Purnells, Whaleys, *et al*, tell their own story of life and death over three centuries on the seaside. Grave sites also tell us about those young wives who died in childbirth years ago, infants who never made it through their first episode of flu or whooping cough, and farmers and watermen who met premature occupation-related deaths.

And look beyond these formal cemeteries, where whole communities attend the passing of one of their own. On the next ramble down a country road, look over in the farmers' fields, where there may be a rise of land and a small group of crosses standing atop, in isolation, the resting place of generations of the landowners. The rise of land serves a purpose: to protect the pine coffins from popping out of the ground, as the wet seasons of the year might otherwise push a typically high water table right up through the top soil along with the coffins and ancestral bones. Even after death, local geography continues to affect human destiny.

Photo by the author

Mayfields: 1683-1970

Mayfields farm was patented in 1683. The rare windmill-powered grist mill and residence were built in the early 1800s. Joshua Carey, Neath Carey's hoary-bearded father, stands imposingly in the windmill opening. Neither mill nor house remained when the author's brother sold Mayfields in 1970.

Photo (mill) circa 1910: collection of Ned Carey
Photo (farmhouse) circa 1940: collection of the author

A Lifetime on the Bay

The Careys were born soon after the Civil War and lived through two world wars and the Great Depression. Electricity finally arrived in 1939. The weekly trip to church in Berlin, over dusty and rutted dirt roads, took nearly an hour each way by horse and carriage. Hard cash for the church collection plate might come from a small life-saving service pension or from the sale of a few logs from the farm. Property taxes took the rest. A doctor in time of need was rare. Yet the Careys truly believed that life was grand—that it could not be any better.

Waiting for Friends on the Front Stoop

A Day on the Bay

Photos: collection of the author

Fishing aboard the *Addie Byrd*, Neath anchors up at his favorite deep-water hole, over an oyster-shell bottom, just off the marsh bank.

The Ultimate Progger

A day of duck hunting with Neath was a prized invitation. The rich and famous came from afar. Black ducks were plentiful along the marsh, especially at first light and at dusk. When the mid-winter freeze would set in, Carey's cove would fill with canvasbacks, redheads, bluebills, and whistlers.

Photos by Purnell Benson, 1936: author's collection

Last Tribute to a Remarkable Lady

Ned Carey preserves a memory on the stern of his commercial fishing boat.

Photo by the author, 2004

IX

What is progress, good or bad?
The red-tailed hawk has been through this fad;
once the barnyard chicken killer,
now the rodent ridder and farmers' pillar,
and that is progress.

Post-World War II: Bridges of Change

Nearing the midpoint of the twentieth century, social development along Maryland's coastal bays entered another time warp. All that had gone on before happened in slow motion, a century at a time: until after World War II, the mule and plow still tilled the fields; social gatherings were dressy affairs; and the beach had yet to become T-shirt city. After almost 100 years, Ocean City extended a mere dozen blocks northward up the beach, while nearby inland communities were undergoing a downward drift in population.

Such was the laid-back pace of life described only a decade earlier by a visiting observer (taken from *Worcester County, Maryland: A Guide to the Old Line State*):

"Worcester County, despite its age in settlement, retains many qualities of its early frontier days. Isolated by geography and until recently by poor roads, the people lived to themselves, indifferent to events in other parts of Maryland, resenting any 'meddling' from Annapolis or Baltimore, obeying the laws they respect, and ignoring those they disapprove. The speech of cultured as well as uncultured persons is spiced with archaic words and phrases. The peculiar emphatic rhythm and slurring of common speech sometimes makes it unintelligible to a Baltimorean."

Irene Williams (THM: 1995)

This is something that happened the last year that I was at the tavern (Williams Tavern, Berlin). I was in the kitchen and the girl that was taking care of the package store came to me and she said, "You better go out to the bar. I think there is going to be a problem." Okay, I go out there and everybody just sitting there, and I know everybody there, and so I said to her, "Who was it?" And she said, "That guy there." And it was A.J. Ketterman. I walked up to him and I said, "A.J., did you just have a problem with somebody"—because I've never had a problem. He said, "Miss Irene, I'm just telling these guys about painting in Ocean City today, and this lady asked me where I was from, was I born here." And I said "yes" and she says, "Hah, everybody down here was inbred until the bay bridge." He was highly indignant and I said, "Oh, A.J., she's got that all wrong. It all started with World War II."

True, war experiences and travels to distant lands by a generation of young men and women had greatly altered connections with the outside world. However, the ensuing influx of new residents and the vast increase in tourism may be seen as the more dramatic catalysts in a visually changing seaside. These latter changes are largely a story about bridges. Modern transportation had at last overcome the centuries of isolation.

In 1952, the Chesapeake Bay Bridge was completed. The historical seaward-vision of coastal bays natives now turned westward toward the stream of automobiles, tourists, property-seekers, and fast-talking investors—the "Come Heres"—all streaming into their watershed from the once far-away western shore. Ocean City was the destination, and the beach resort quickly expanded another 200 blocks to connect with the smaller Delaware resort of Fenwick. High-rise condominiums were soon to follow, replacing family cottages, colonnaded apartments, and shingle-sided hotels as the latest architectural model along the beach front.

Harry Wimbrow (TP: 2004)

I had to move my (roadside produce) stand this summer. Land got sold for a new development. I've got this spot for maybe 2-3 years, and then it'll probably be gone, too. Maybe then, I'll just pull everything back to the farm (in Whaleyville) and settle in.

I can hardly believe it. The traffic out here along 589 has gotten so bad, you're just about to get crushed. And now look at Berlin; it's soon gonna be connected to Ocean City, all the new development around there. I drive the school bus past that new project on Decatur Farm. One day there's a field and the next day there's this whole new stack of boxes out there, homes sprouting up like blades of grass.

You were asking about hog killing? I haven't done that in fifteen years. We used to do it all—making the sausage and scrapple and smoking the bacon and hams. Maybe we ought to do another. I have to get some people together, those that know how are scarce now and they live in what you might call the backwoods. We'll get some hogs with fat on them, not those lean things, the supermarket variety that's all lean and no flavor. Our parents' generation, they liked that layer of fat on the outside that tastes

> **good, gives the meat some flavor. The sort of thing that the doctors say will kill you. I don't know; a lot of their generation lived to near a hundred.**

In short order, Worcester County was divided into separate cultures, and the contrasting social spheres exist to this day. One Worcester County is contained in the urbanizing northeastern quadrant comprising Ocean City, West Ocean City, and Ocean Pines. Here, the population is growing at a faster rate than anywhere else in Maryland, and development is straining to burst out of this upper-outer quadrant and overflow along the approaching highways. The other quadrants range inland and down the coastal bays to include more stable historic communities, farmlands, forests, and, what this account addresses, the natural undeveloped reaches of the lower coastal bays.

The second eventful bridge, the Verrazano Bridge, spanning the Sinepuxent Bay was built in 1962, opening Assateague Island to the flood of traffic at a time when commercial development of the island seemed imminent. Adding to human pressures on the island, a bridge was also built a year later between Chincoteague Island and the mainland, both of which accelerated growth of that community and offered the prospect of linking the Virginia and Maryland portions of the island with a paved highway.

Yet another bridge would add to the human influx. In 1963 the Chesapeake Bay-Tunnel Bridge connected the Eastern Shore of Virginia with Norfolk, encouraging a flow of traffic from New York and New Jersey through the Delmarva Peninsula. Travelers along this north-south route—abetted by a new ferry connection between Cape May, New Jersey, and Lewes, Delaware—liked what they saw. Driving through unspoiled country, many would pull over and put down permanent roots.

Depending on one's point of view, these last fifty years have been either the best or the worst of times. Prosperity dominates much of the landscape. Recreational opportunities have dramatically expanded for vacationers as well as local day-trippers. The Assateague parks have complemented the more urbanized vacation attractions of Ocean City, together hosting millions of visitors annually. Surely tourism can be a clean business—potentially one of the least threatening to a community's heritage and natural assets. But the very number of people sends out strong signals of alarm.

Among the positive changes has been the belated recognition of the role of the black community in local history. After nearly a century, Civil War issues were at last being muted by the influx of new residents, increasing tourism and economic development, and civil rights legislation. In retrospect, the Civil War may be remembered foremost for its divisiveness, especially on the Eastern Shore. Maryland was a border, slave-holding state, yet officially loyal to the Union. Many on the Eastern Shore sympathized with the Confederacy; yet, sons and brothers sometimes went off to enlist in opposite camps. For both free and enslaved blacks, however, there was an obvious choice.

Isaiah Fassett and his three brothers were granted freedom from slavery on a plantation in Sinepuxent on the condition they join the Union Army. The government paid the slaveholder $300 for each recruit—part of an aggressive Union campaign to sign up African-Americans to join the regiments of the U.S. Colored Troop. Fassett and his colleagues performed on the front lines in the taking of Richmond by the Union Army, as well as in subsequent battles through the South. In 1944, Fassett, still spry and alert, was honored at age 100 as Worcester County's last surviving veteran of the Civil War. He had established a tradition of commitment to military duty in the black community that has endured through two world wars and up to the present time.

World War II Revisited
Joe Purnell (THM: 1995)

...The colonel had us all assembled and he said, "Mens, this is it. People in the States have been thinking about the 366th," and why he says they know how it is, "because you are all black. And, mens, we're going to go up there at night...and remember one thing—your M-1. That's your rifle will be your mama, the bayonet will be your baby sister...we'll move up tonight and don't think the Germans don't know you're coming, 'cause they do; they're watchin' in. Now some of you are going to go up there and you're not going to be coming back." And Olin (buddy) said to me, "Joe, I'm one of them not comin' back." But I said to him, "Man, I'm coming back." "Joe," he says, "when you get to tell my Mom that I've got $10,000 for her, and Mom, that little house you wanted, I want you to take that $10,000 and I want you to buy that house." And Duncan (another buddy) also said, "Joe, I'm not going back either." And they were up on the front lines, but they got dead, Duncan and Olin.

Anyway, I got out of there and I remember a colonel was coming down and he asked me if I was going down to the hospital. All I could say was, "Cap, Cap, Cap," and he said, "Can you make it?" I was at the 31st General Hospital...pretty near four weeks, and I had a friend named Roy from Macon, Georgia. Roy said to me one time, "You know something, Purnell...I was taught by my parents that a negro was no good, but they taught me wrong. When I go back home, I'm changing." and I said, "Roy, you know what? That 88 gun didn't say, Roy, you're white or Joe, you're black. That 88 just would kill you."

I got three battle stars and each star showed that I was in combat and each star represents the battle I was in. Congressman Bauman had me come up to his office in Washington, D.C., and we walked over to this place and Senator Brooks pinned this bronze star on me.

"We Shall Overcome," the most popular folk song of all time has a gospel ring of both heartache and aspiration. That may be because Pete Seeger, the dean of folk artists, adapted the song from the hymn, "I'll Overcome Someday," a composition by the inspiring Charles Tindley. Born in Berlin in 1856 and orphaned at an early age, Tindley rose to become one of the most popular preachers of his time. Tindley escaped a childhood of dirt-farm poverty and illiteracy, taught himself to read the Bible before he knew his ABCs, and made his way to Philadelphia, where he became janitor of the Bainbridge Street Methodist Church.

Self-educated, the magnetic Tindley would soon become minister of the church with all 130 members. Thirty-one years later, his multiracial congregation numbered over 12,000, the largest congregation of its kind in the United States. In 1982, some fifty years after his death, Tindley was honored by the Smithsonian Institution as the father of gospel music. Tindley had been multi-talented, prolific, and one of a kind. Today, the Tindley Temple in Philadelphia carries on his work.

Deep religious faith, a trait of the traditional black community, may be seen as a driving force behind the exploits of other notable achievers. Elijah Johnson, a runaway slave from a farm near Snow Hill, received international recognition as "the great Liberian hero." Prior to the American Civil War Johnson joined a ship of free blacks who were being relocated to Africa as an experiment by the U.S. Government and the American Colonization Society to repatriate former slaves to the home of their ancestors. Johnson subsequently led the colonization of Liberia, defending Americo-Liberians against warring local tribes and establishing both Christianity and the foundation of a new nation. His son, H.R.W. Johnson, later became the first president of the Republic of Liberia, the only independent Black African state for another 100 years. In the twenty-first century another revolution in this allied nation is headline news, although the story of its Americo-Liberian origin has been relegated to a footnote.

A strong relationship has remained between the descendants of the Liberian colonists and their relatives in the Berlin-Snow Hill area. Out of this relationship comes yet another familiar story of "hardship to fame"—that of Sarah Henry Cyrus. After leaving the United Methodist Church community of Berlin in her youth, Sarah Cyrus earned her degree in nursing in Philadelphia, followed the trail to Liberia, and headed a Christian mission for nearly fifty years. She was honored many times for her missionary work.

Over the years, much of the black community has moved away from the farm. Tenant farmers have entered professions, won elected offices, opened small businesses, and managed larger ones. Yet, this is but a segment of the minority community that tends to stand apart, whether from a continued feeling of estrangement or simply from a sense of comfort with what is familiar.

Such heritage might be interpreted from the paintings of prominent local artist Patrick Henry, whether or not this is a conscious intention. A soft, mellow light washes Henry's scenes of isolated rural homesteads set on wooded lots. Little sign of life is visible, except, perhaps, the wash hanging bleach-white on a clothesline or the faint flicker of light from a TV set inside a darkened home. Paint-peeling rowboats lie abandoned on the edge of the marsh. Village streets are nearly empty, and white people with blank faces often appear to be idle. On the other hand, natural landscapes and seascapes beckon and burst with vitality and a golden glow that distinguish Henry from his peers. Henry's close-up portraits of black figures are also right on. There is much that can be read into the simplest canvas.

An Artist Reminisces
Patrick Henry (NPS: 2004)

I began drawing almost before I remember. I may have been about five when I took an old pie plate, drew a circle, and remember filling it in with eyes...Actually that pivotal point came when I was in high school. In the 10th grade we had a student exhibition and it was actually an abstract experimental thing that I had in the show. I always did representations, but this new art teacher came in fresh out of college and wanted us to extend our imaginations...So I did this abstract painting and I sold it. And I said, "Ooh, this is nice. I can do something that I love and make money from it." I was sixteen, so that was closing in on forty years now of pure struggle to build a career where your work is respected, collected, desired—which you can't even put into words.

It was after this transition in '75 that a collector, through word of mouth, wanted to meet me and see my art work. He was a very successful real estate developer and he had the means to not only purchase my work but also to challenge me to break free of this

introverted servitude mentality. What I had to do in his words was "toot my own horn," because he said no one else would do it for you. And that was very difficult because for years the whole creative process in a way is a sort of self-edification. It's about pulling that out what's deep within, and to not only do that but also to talk about it was very difficult. And at times it still is.

In African society, because there was no printing, the passing down of history was through the most elderly, men or women, and they called them—I want to say the terms is "Griat"—and they would be powerful storytellers. They received stories from their ancestors and they would gather around, I would imagine, campfires and (go) from village to village. When you imagine that the society was not distracted by outside influences, these messages could become very powerful. This was passed on to generations and I think my mother received it.

When I was in college in 1972...I drew a portrait of this old black gentleman with an old cowboy type hat, white, white beard and hair, and dark skin with a powerful glistening glance at you—though his eyes were that watery, a little reddish, off-tinted white in the eyes. And when I brought the painting home, Mom said it looked just like her great grandfather and his name was Guess Parker. I said, "Mom, how do you spell it." GUESS. And the interesting story was that as a little child Mom remembered Grandpa Guess and she was a little bit afraid of him because he would tell stories of his past, coming over on the slave ship. And a lot of these stories were filtered with ghosts and witchcraft and that type of thing. But it really had a powerful influence. And I believe that gift of dialogue passed through my mother, 'cause my mother could remember specific details in her family's life. And she's passed it on to her children.

Now, another burgeoning minority group is making its presence felt—the Hispanic community. Fifty years or more ago, migrant Hispanic workers descended on Delmarva to pick the cucumbers, tomatoes, strawberries, sweet corn, and the peach crops. Then the migrant workers departed. The crops they harvested, and the canneries that packed the produce, had moved elsewhere. The Hispanic community, Central Americans, would re-emerge, however, with the construction boom and, by all appearances, settle down permanently. Many are establishing their own businesses—landscaping, masonry work, and fast-food Mexican eateries. A few have bought their own patch of farmland, raising produce where their parents had earned bare wages in the fields a generation before. Likely, the development of Hispanic roots along the coastal bays will be the subject of heritage preservation projects in the next generation.

The commercial harbor behind Ocean City, at the top of Sinepuxent Bay, is one place to observe one era giving way to another. Over the past sixty years or more, the harbor has been a busy home of ocean-fishing trawlers and wholesale and retail fish markets. Watermen have lived in modest dwellings around the harbor. Retired fishing skiffs could find a home and rot away on any number of vacant lots. Land was cheap. The charm of a robust fishing community was dear. Now look around the harbor and spot the latest fashions. Expensive sportfishing boats are well-tended in private marinas. Restaurants are moving upscale. Fishermen's cottages and shacks are being replaced by luxury townhouses. Undoubtedly, there's more to come.

Ride down Route 611 and South Point Road and, in the same vein, observe the new communities resting on the soy bean and corn fields of a few years ago and the few remaining plantation-era homes standing next to the architectural styles of today. The 1732 dwelling, Genesar, near the end of Sinepuxent Neck, is a good example of that. The Rackliffe House, stranded for some time in the middle of Rum Pointe Golf Course, is another.

Inland settlements have provided more promising examples of local traditions competing with changes in economic forces. Berlin, a historic gateway to the beaches, has taken a new lease on life by doing its best not to change. To walk along Main Street is to ply the same path taken by the Assateague Indians and, later, colonial stage coaches. Lined up harmoniously along Main Street today are neatly-kept residences that date from several distinct architectural periods. Elegant Federal mansions sit next to cross-gabled Victorian homes, flanked by distinctive twentieth century cottages and 4-square designs. Older residences may display non-functioning vestiges of an agricultural past. Smokehouses, corn cribs, dairies, and even the obsolete privy may be viewed on a walk about town. One of the finest sets of out-buildings in the county is located at the rear of Robin's Nest—formerly known as the Whaley House—located on the corner of Broad and West Streets.

Halfway along Main Street, the historic commercial district imposes its neat, uniformly-brick construction in the center of town—a model of small-scale, late-Victorian design for downtown business centers. The nostalgia prompted by this village atmosphere has made Berlin a tourist destination and has attracted the production of two major studio movies. Historic preservation has proven to be a good strategy for revitalizing such communities.

So it goes elsewhere in the county. North on Rt. 113, the vintage settlements of Bishopville and Showell are showing signs of coming to life. On the edge of Showell, St. Martin's Episcopal Church, built in 1757-1762, is an exquisitely preserved example of the Anglican tradition. Its doors have now been reopened for special events, ecumenical services, garden tours, and other visitations by appointment.

Farther south, along Rt. 113 below Berlin, Snow Hill and Pocomoke City boast even older examples of their architectural heritage. Situated just outside the coastal watershed, along the Pocomoke River, these historic towns share a similar legacy of social development. As elsewhere, the challenge is to preserve the significant sites before they disappear. Another aim is to guide new construction to harmonize with period-style architecture of the past. To this end the County Commissioners have voted to maintain a scenic corridor along Rt. 113, and to establish voluntary guidelines for new construction that reflect the vernacular architectural heritage.

Visitors can play a significant role in the ongoing debate on balancing growth with environment considerations. While residents are counted in the thousands, visitors number in the millions and provide most of the county's revenue. But they may cease to visit the area if the waters are degraded and over-development impacts the region's natural attractions. Hence, interest in preserving the resources of the coastal bays is now a part of the mainstream of public discussion. No longer does one hear automatically the comment, "Well, you can't stop progress," in reference to land-development projects and the effects on water quality in the coastal bays of pollutants from construction projects, golf courses, agricultural practices, and recreational activities. A consensus in the community is coming to understand the trade-offs. The connections between natural resource protection, preservation of cultural and social traditions, and sustainable economic development, as promised with heritage-oriented tourism, are still recent concepts.

For those who would like to put their concern for environmental values into action, participation is invited by a number of local organizations advocating sustainable management of the bays' resources. Assateague Coastal Trust (ACT), a private non-profit organization, has for more than thirty years been a conservation watchdog—seeing that government officials and agencies keep their promises to the environment. The charter members of ACT (formerly the Committee for Preservation of Assateague) were in the forefront of lobbying Congress to establish Assateague Island National Seashore Park. ACT has enlarged its mission to include hands-on programs for restoring oysters in the coastal bays, protecting threatened species such as the diamondback terrapin, developing public awareness programs, and actively advocating against destructive development practices.

In 2002, ACT joined hands with the Waterkeeper Alliance, a national organization recognized for its role in cleaning up the Hudson River, San Francisco Bay, and other bodies of water throughout the country. Under ACT's auspices, this has become known as the Assateague Coastkeeper program and has gained attention for its advocacy of coastal bays protection.

The Maryland Coastal Bays Program (MCBP), part of the National Estuary Program established by Congress in 1987, has made a critical contribution by providing a comprehensive management plan for protecting natural resources that ultimately affect the coastal bays. Significantly, this management plan is supported by all levels of government and is a key reference for land-use planning in Worcester County. A Citizens Advisory Committee, addressing ongoing coastal bays-related issues, meets regularly and is open to public participation. The Coastal Bays Foundation is a private non-profit arm of MCBP, with a mission of raising funds to support operations and to provide grants for worthy projects to individuals and organizations in the community.

D-LITE (Delmarva Low-Impact Tourism Experiences) has been formed locally to establish and promote environmentally-responsible tourism. The organization's progress has been remarkable, as its development of birding, biking, and canoeing adventures has rapidly gained national attention. The most recent creation of D-LITE, the Delmarva Alliance for Bicycling, is offering a "Bicyclists Guide to Delmarva," which maps over 2,000 miles of rural trails through cypress swamp, farmland, tidal marsh, and coastal plain forest from the C & D Canal to Cape Charles, Virginia.

Since, geographically, these excursions are readily accessible to one-third of the nation's population, care is taken to stress the "low-impact" ethic: leave no footprints. While D-LITE has initially aimed at giving its seal of approval to those responsible businesses directly associated with ecotourism—such as camping, canoeing, biking, birdwatching, and generally progging around—the broader goal is to gain support from the mainstream tourism industry concerning reduced consumption of the coastal bays' natural resources.

The Lower Eastern Shore Heritage Council (LESHC) is also a partner in sustaining traditional cultural values of the three lower shore counties—Worcester, Somerset, and Wicomico. LESHC is especially active in preserving, protecting, and promoting historic sites. The mission of LESHC includes promotion of the arts and crafts of the region, as well as the heritage tourism opportunities.

In addition to these contributing organizations and agencies has been the on-going support of a few visionary politicians and individuals who began to fight the environmental battle before the cause was popular. Especially noteworthy has been a half-century of dedicated effort by Ilia Fehrer, recognized as one of the country's outstanding advocates of environmental protection. Fehrer was an instrumental voice in the community for establishing the Assateague Island National Seashore and, over the years, in supporting growth management and anti-pollution policies in the coastal bays watershed.

One voice can make a difference.

Patrick Henry at work in his studio in Berlin, capturing the heritage of the coastal bays like no other artist.

Photo by the author

Main Street in Berlin, Circa 1900 (Top) and 1992 (Bottom)

Except for paved streets and automobiles, much has remained the same. Preservation of this heritage has served as a successful strategy for revitalizing the commercial center and creating new demand for residential homes.

Collection of the author

Historic Berlin Walking Tour

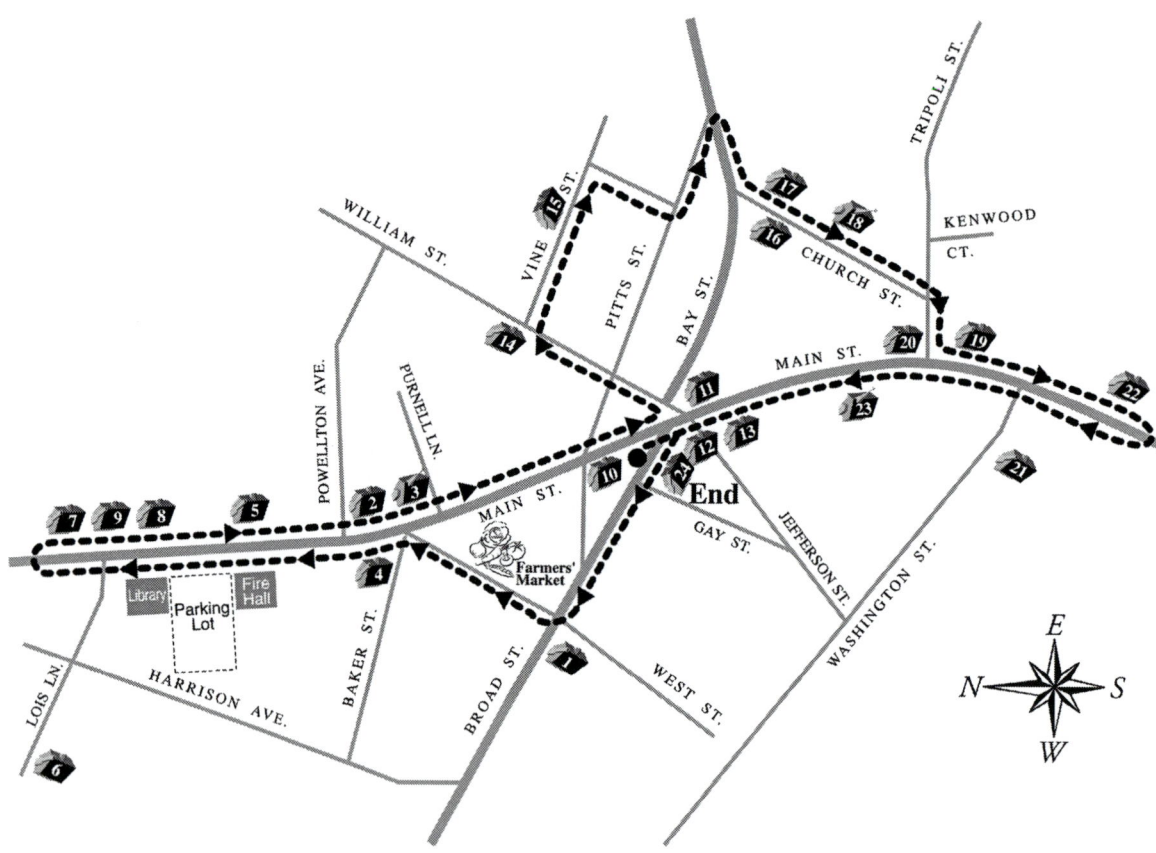

1. Whaley House or "Robin's Nest"
2. Stevenson House
3. Stevenson Methodist Church
4. Calvin B. Taylor House Museum
5. George Harrison House
6. Orlando Harrison House
7. William Nelson House
8. Queen Anne Style House
9. Presbyterian Manse
10. Calvin B. Taylor House
11. Peninsula Bank
12. Atlantic Hotel
13. Old Paran Lodge
14. Pitts Family House
15. "Telescope House"
16. David Truitt House (Two-Part Frame Dwelling)
17. "Littleworth"
18. St. Paul's Episcopal Church
19. Kenwood
20. Site of Burley Inn
21. John T. Keas House
22. Burley Cottage
23. Buckingham Presbyterian Church
24. Globe Theater

X

When the mosquitoes and flies drone by
enough to make a grown man cry,
the ponies just switch their tails,
while over the flats the swallows and bats
feed on the skeeters and no-see-'ems.

Assateague Island Off-Beat Experiences

Less than 50 years ago, a surf fisherman or duck hunter could drive his dune buggy along Assateague Island from the Ocean City Inlet to the barrier fence at the Virginia line without crossing the tracks of more than a handful of other souls of his kind, plus, on a fair day, a real estate salesman, with a customer or two in tow, talking up the promise of a wondrous new resort that was not to be. Within the span of a generation, the Assateague Island seashore parks would become a jewel in the crown of the nation's public beaches. Millions now visit the island annually to enjoy any number of outdoor experiences that make this destination the hub of ecotourism on Maryland's seaside.

Fully ninety-nine percent of the visitors to the Maryland portion of the island partake in the user-friendly activities that are easily accessible from Bayberry Drive, the public road to life-guarded beaches and the beach- and bay-side campgrounds. There is something for everybody: sunning, surfing in the brisk ocean, or lowering one's bones in the bathtub-warm waters of the bay; beachcombing alone or taking any of various nature or local history walks led by park service interpreters; watching wildlife and birding along one of the premier summer nesting and wintering stations of migratory shore birds; fishing, clamming, crabbing; and paddling a canoe around Bird Island or voyaging through the maze of marsh-rimmed sloughs and guts as far as energy, tide, and weather allow. The visitor can explore these and other opportunities through the Barrier Island Visitors Center, located at the foot of the Verrazano Bridge, or at the Chincoteague National Wildlife Refuge Visitors Center at the Virginia end of the island, or through their web sites.

The Virginia section of Assateague Island, encompassing both an extension of the National Seashore Park and the Chincoteague National Wildlife Refuge Center, draws a similar number of visitors as the Maryland portion. All are part of the "Assateague Experience." These are superb attractions less than an hour's drive from Ocean City, and belonging to the same watershed.

Yet it is for that other one percent—the most hardy, adventuresome, and nostalgic—that Assateague Island offers another dimension of escape: a priceless remoteness away from the pack. Nearly two-thirds of the Maryland stretch is removed from private vehicular traffic and is preserved in much the same condition as when the explorer Giovanni da Verrazano briefly disembarked on the beach almost 500 years ago and called this wild and forested land the new Arcadia. From the northern tip of the island to the Verrazano Bridge, seven miles of washed-over, shell-pocked sand and patches of scrub vegetation are reachable by walk-in and boat-in only; and boat-in by deep-drafted craft is practical only at the very tip next to Ocean City Inlet. The extremely shallow waters of the bay behind the island take care of that. But what a grand way to pass the day on a hiking or surf-fishing excursion along this stretch, so devoid of trampling that the endangered piping plover, shy of human presence and the very icon of nature preservation, has established one of its major nesting sites. Here, the beach-walker may stumble across the remains of an old wreck, or a sea turtle searching a nesting site, an assortment of seashells, sightings of various shore birds, bald eagles and marsh-preying hawks...all in a morning's hike that few others are likely to be sharing.

The "back-country" of Assateague Island resumes farther south, beyond the popular bathing beaches and the last parking lot. Although 4-wheel-drive vehicles are allowed along the surf bank, traffic is closed to the trails behind that lead into the more primitive forest and marsh communities, which appear untouched except for the vacant remains of one-time gunning shanties. There is little coastal wilderness like it left in the country. It is strictly backpack-in or paddle through the bay-shallows to find a rare solid landing. For this, a depth chart of the Chincoteague Bay and some help from the Park Service or a local guide is highly recommended to find one's way past the Egging Beaches to Lumber Marsh, Beacon Clump, Pirates Islands, Striking Marsh, and Pope Island. The names embody much of the human history of the island and are enough to invite the intrepid paddler and wilderness camper.

Tackling the bay-side and back-country of Assateague in the height of summer can be daunting when the air is still or a land-breeze brings out the insects in full force; for this reason, the cooler months may be preferable to foray through marsh and forest by those who are especially bug-sensitive. Although the mosquitoes and greenhead flies are notorious, the black, or gray, fly is the acme of pestilence. Simple advice here is to dress for the occasion, the same way previous generations did, with protective clothing. Bikinis, short pants, short-sleeved shirts or bare chests don't work.

The best garb for man, woman, and child are long pants, such as well-worn khakis, a long-sleeved cotton dress shirt that has been retired from serious wear, an auxiliary pair of old tennis shoes that can be worn in and out of the bay, and a broad-brimmed hat, preferably on the order of a straw sombrero. There's not much skin left exposed for the mosquitoes and flies to target. Insect repellent, if any, can be restricted to a few dabs on exposed skin surfaces. If this outfit is kept on throughout the waking hours, on a hiking trail or while progging around the marsh and in the bay, the bug problem is minimal. Like the Arab dressed in long robes to protect from the desert heat, the properly dressed camper can also maintain a similar dead-air space between the skin and outer garment that insulates against the enemies to human life at the beach.

In the fall of the year, on a blustery day, the place to have once been in the back-country of Assateague was in any of the private gunning clubs, which have now been vacated by their former owners and sit idly along the edges of the marsh. The names of these hunting retreats are enough to conjure up a vision of life on the bay in earlier times: High Winds, Green Run Lodge, Pope Island Gun Club, and Bob-O-Del, to identify just a few. May these old lodges be saved for a time yet, if only to assuage those who have appreciated when the wind comes nor'west and the waterfowl were scudding across the bay and a warm fire was waiting inside. This is a heritage that deserves preservation in some form or other. That duck blinds are still maintained by the Park Service for public use has been a measure welcomed by local sportsmen.

Gunning Club Recollections
Joseph Hickmott, Jr. (NPS:1986)

Assateague in the late 20s was quite different than it is now...I counted over six: they were called gun clubs. They were not called hunting clubs. Most of the gun clubs on Assateague were set up by men from Berlin...it wasn't until about the mid-30s that another group from Ocean City got involved in a gun club (Green Run). They were the Jackson boys...and they had fine facilities. They advertised hunting and they brought in a lot of personalities at that particular time—the Philadelphia Athletics owned by Connie Mack. Their baseball players would come down here to hunt: Jimmy Foxx, Bob Grove, George M. Shaw, Howard Ehmke, Mickey Cochrane, Joe Boley, Bing Miller, etc. They would come down when they weren't playing and would hunt for ducks and geese.

Kendall Jarvis (NPS: 1987)

...There were other properties used mainly for hunting and fishing recreation. First was the High Winds, which was originally bought by Mr. Glen Riddle, who came here in about 1918. Then other properties: Purnell's at Troy Slough, Sugar Hill Slough and at Cedar Valley.

The first organized division of properties on the beach...I recall was when Glen Riddle came here and bought an estate. He was owner of Man O' War,...a famous race horse. (Riddle) began to, as you could then, take up land which was just state land, get a patent or deed to it and post it so no one else could hunt. He took up an enormous section of land, some four or five miles of bay front, from approximately North Beach to almost Green Run. Local people, then wondering what to do to preserve their rights, took all the off-shore islands off the points which (Riddle) had taken. This action forced Mr. Riddle into a compromise and so the land was split.

Milton Cooper (TP:2004)

Norman Calhoun had a cabin, became a gunnin' club. There were four or five houses in the yard of the Pope's Island Station. Norman bought the best one and moved it a mile or so up the beach and set it down along the drain there.

If you only killed 15 or 20 bluebills, it wasn't a good day....25 or 30 was a normal day's shooting. Norman was down there gunning one day and the bluebills never showed up. But the game wardens did. They used to fly around in an airplane and they'd taxi right up and land. They got smart after awhile. They knew we didn't feed 'em in front of the blind. They'd go out back of the blind and pull a drag. This one day he found some corn back of the blind...plane taxied right up and the warden was standing right out on the pontoons. "Boys," he said, "I've found something. It don't look too good." And you know what Sid (Bennett) said to the warden? "Well, *you* found it. That's more than the ducks did."

In Memory of Norman E. Calhoun, 1892-1975
Penned by his Son (Courtesy of Milton Cooper)

This log of Calhoun's Lodge (edited portion) beginning in 1948 and ending in 1962 describes and records the glorious days of Duck and Geese hunting on Assateague Island, Va.-Md. It has planted within our minds the seeds of good relationship with our hunting pals and fostered everlasting friendship to all those who shot with us at the lodge. It brings back fond memories of some of the finest wildfowl shooting any duck hunter might seek to enjoy.

We pay tribute and respect to Orville Quillen, Bill Jester, Wyle Maddox, Lou Conklin, John Dukes, The Bay Ferry (Harry Gunby and Jack "Pot Pie" Purnell, The Popes Island Gunning Club, the Popes Island Coast Guard, to Ed Duffy, Cale Boggs, Don Simplerton, to Jim Williams and Herb Buckalew, to Leonard Savage and Marvin Watson, and to all of those who we knew as Assateague gunners and fishermen.

There are those who gave use the delicious meals, especially those steaming oyster stews which warmed our bellies after a cold morning's shoot. To Harry West, Nelson Dolby and Mrs. Norman E. Calhoun, we say *Thank You and God Bless You All.* There are those who contributed and made Calhoun's our second home. Ed Graef, Sid Bennett, Dr. Wm. Campbell and Milt Cooper. To them we say, *Thank You So Much.*

Memories of the splendid days spent on Popes Is. will remain in our hearts forever. We sincerely hope that our Sons, Grandsons, and their Sons can someday enjoy the same shooting pleasure we had on Assateague. May my Dad, in his final resting place, be enjoying the memories of shooting his favorite duck–The Canvasback.

Norman C. Calhoun, 7-10-75

J. D. Quillin (NPS: 1987)

I started going to Assateague Island when I was about five years old, round 1941. It was a big adventure. My dad was a member of a gunning club called Bob-O'-Del. Josh Bunting was the guide at the time…one evening he took me out after dinner and he asked me, "You want to go somewhere?" I said, "Sure." So he took me out and said, "We're going snipe hunting." He took me down to the other end of the main island and gave me a bag and told me what a snipe looked like—like a little yellowleg. I was supposed to catch 'im, throw the bag over and catch 'im and put 'im in the bag. He left me out there. I thought I stayed forever; probably I stayed a half an hour. I didn't know if he was ever going to come back for me. So I was roaming all over looking for snipes. Finally he came back and wanted to know if I had caught any. I said, "No, I didn't see any, let alone catch 'em."

Anyway, I took a lot of people snipe hunting after that. No one ever seemed to catch any snipes, but we had a good time.

Surf fishing is permitted all along the island, except in crowded bathing areas under the protection of lifeguards. But these are usually not the best fishing spots in any case, regardless of season. The true surf fisherman is looking for those more distant sloughs between offshore sand bar and beach where the big red drum and ocean-run stripers and bluefish school up in the spring and fall. The time is usually early morning or in the late afternoon and well into the evening, as the tide rises and after the sun goes down. The enjoyment is not, for some, in the numbers of fish caught. It's also tailgating with a view to the horizon over the mesmerizing rise and fall of the sea, with much to think about and be grateful for. Nearly a century ago Frank Stick painted and wrote, perhaps better than anyone, about the pleasures of barrier islands. He penned some words in *Call of the Surf* (1920) that were prophetic and as timely as yesterday:

"Game and fish are fast disappearing as our remoter sections become settled, as lakes and bayous are drained, and I have been assured that the time is not far distant when we will have degenerated into a race of stoop-shouldered anaemic creatures, fit only for such mild recreative pastimes as bridge whist contests and pink teas...I would hate to think of my children, and of my children's children being deprived of those healthful, zestful, and entirely innocent recreations...which have done so much to make this very earthly sphere of ours such an entirely satisfactory dwelling place...You will still have the spray in your face and the salt breeze will come sweet to your nostrils, yet the clean sand will be beneath your feet. The vasty deep will roll before your eyes, and the blue sky will arch above your head...yet storm, or wind, or rain, shall hold no terrors for you.

"The fascination of our environments, the widespread ocean, changing constantly with every hour that passes, and with each slightest fluctuation in wind or tide; the wide, clean beach; the broken dunes; and the salt grass, giving to the constant breeze...If you are a fisherman, and follow the call of the surf, you will come to know and care for it all with an instinctive appreciation, such as I suppose as the gray gull feels as he wheels in the wind, and blends his cry with the voice of the waters."

Finding that spot on the island where one can be utterly alone can be disconcerting, even troubling, for some visitors. It's not something one may be used to anymore. But for others, this can be a rejuvenating experience.

Fishing the Surf for Drum, Early 1900s

Collection of Roe Terry

Sporting on Assateague Island, 1920 - 2004

Gunning on the coastal bays behind Assateague is the stuff of legend and many tall tales. Visiting sportsmen came from afar to join with local waterfowlers in an age of abundance. The vacated gunning shanties on the island are now the property of the National Park Service. Mobile floating shanties, or houseboats, could be used as overnight living quarters. The old houseboats are still in demand, but hard to find.

Author and his Lab retriever Beau getting ready (left).

Photo by Melville Quillen (c. 1920), collection of the author (top); photo (bottom) by Richard Wechsler, 2004

Two Styles of Old Gunning Clubs on Assateague Island

Bob-O-Del typifies the floating shanties moored permanently to the island and improved by surrounding decks and boat slips.

Clayton Bunting's shingle-sided gunning lodge was built above high water in the vernacular beach style (right). The mid-70s model Jeep Wagoneer signified the nearing end of private hunting rights on the island.

(Top) Collection of the author; (bottom) collection of Melton Cooper

Current Nature-Based Recreational Activities

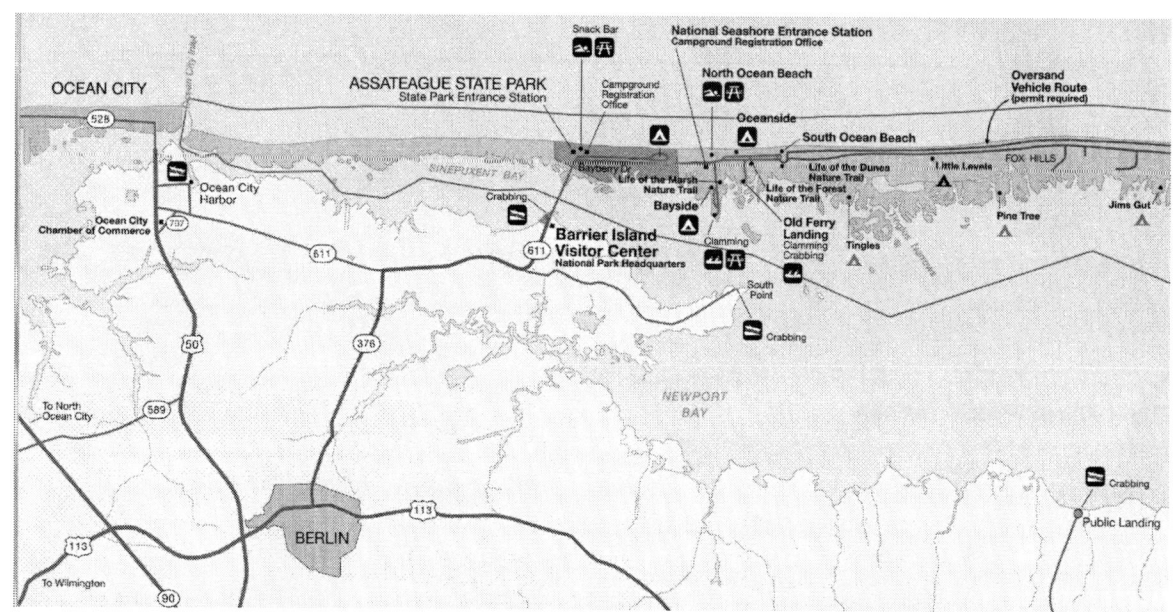

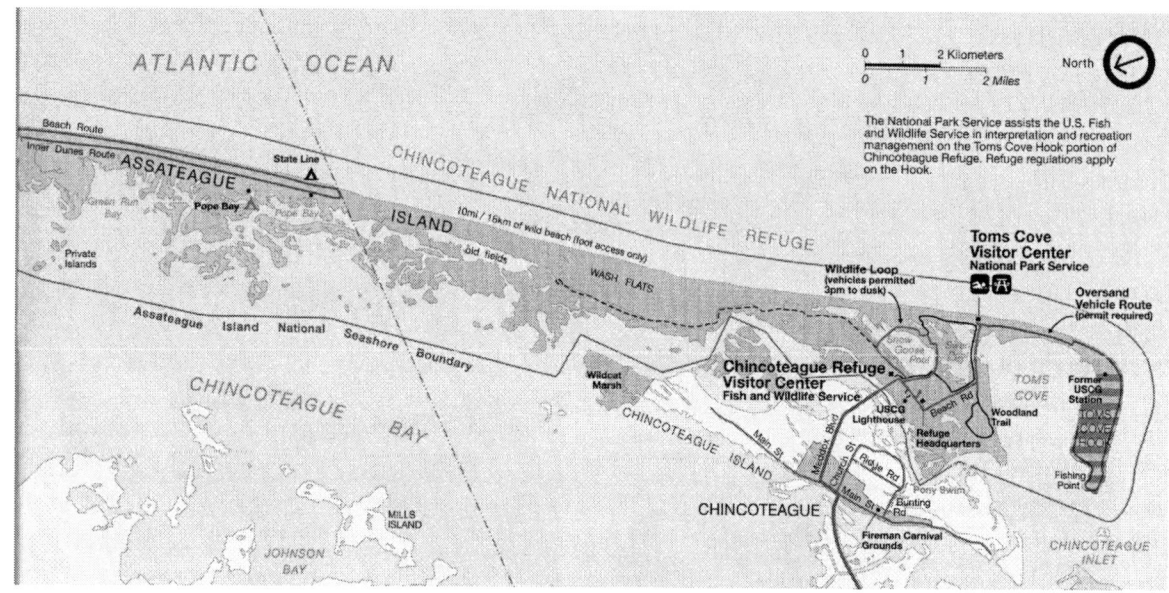

Adapted from the National Park Service brochure

XI

Open space is the precious gift
that lets old Tom strut his stuff,
and free range on the fallen mast
that lies ascatter on the forest floor;
for the good steward, that's enough.

Less-Traveled Byways along the Chincoteague Bay: Villages and Boat Landings Lost in Time

While the northeastern quadrant of Worcester County—Ocean City and its urbanizing spokes on the mainland—has sped into the twenty-first century, the water trails and country byways along the Chincoteague Bay have moved at a different pace. The serenity of this out-of-time tableau casts its charm—a spell waiting to be broken.

The small settlements that spread out over some thirty-five country miles toward the Virginia line were once called Fleaville, Ticktown, Stock Town, Box Iron, Rabbit Knaw, and the like. These original names spoke of the livelihood of watermen and farm workers, of their exposure to the tidewater elements, and of humble dwellings warmed by wood fires and lighted in the evening with candles and nickel kerosene lamps. The small enclaves grew around the settlers' early wood-frame churches, and their village names would undergo as many changes as would their economic fortunes. Currently, with a new generation of place names, these rural settlements have taken on an aura not unlike sleepy Montana mining towns, where initial veins of wealth have been exhausted, yet the potential for new exploration of natural gas lies with considerable promise near the old mine shafts. In rural Worcester County, the analogous situation is a startling find for both historic preservationists and land speculators.

A good starting point for travel and recreation along Chincoteague Bay would be either Berlin or Snow Hill—both worthy of leisurely visits in their own right. Berlin has an advantage of being closer to the flow of traffic from the ocean beaches and is endowed with considerable charm—its Victorian-flavored Main Street with antique and retail shops, good lodgings, and first-class restaurants. Snow Hill is a comparable destination. Although technically situated in the Chesapeake Bay watershed, Snow Hill is located just six miles from Chincoteague Bay. As the county seat, with its wealth of eighteenth and nineteenth century buildings and historic sites, it is also representative of the social heritage of the lower coastal bays.

Leaving Berlin on this particular journey, motorists may head south on Rt. 113. Seven miles down the road, just past the rural village of Newark on the right, the traveler should turn left on either Newark Road or, in another half-mile, on Basket Switch Road. The initial route for the biker (see map) takes a back way out of Berlin that avoids the more traveled Rt. 113 and also winds up at Basket Switch, after a short trip through farmlands and past the recently restored Queponco Railway Station in Newark.

Basket Switch was once a busy shipping point for lumber products. Now the only rail traffic is a semi-weekly haul of chicken feed between the poultry operations in Snow Hill, Berlin, and Showell. The one-time basket factory and brick kiln are long-gone, together with many of the homes that clustered for support around these commercial operations.

The passing of an earlier era will continue to show itself all along the way. Deteriorating houses, abandoned churches, and lifeless farm buildings are common. Exterior white paint has peeled slowly away. Once-generous porches are falling in. It becomes a game to play: recognizing these discarded structures by their nineteenth century features. It can be fun, as children might have counting livestock on passing by roadside pastures.

But what has not been lost by a previous downturn of growth and development is also soon apparent along this sparsely inhabited byway. The lightly trafficked Chincoteague Bay, tiny mainland settlements, and the thousands of acres of marshes, road-lined woodlands, and pancake-flat crop lands compose an unsurpassed tidewater setting. It is hard to come across a single disruptive view, except for dereliction, from Basket Switch to below the Virginia line. Modest hardtop roads wind through the flood plain. Narrow tidewater guts meander away from the bays, dividing fields of corn and soy beans and dead-ending in stands of pine.

Traveling down Cedartown and Taylor Roads, we reach the corner that is recognized on maps as Spence, a loose scattering of less than a dozen homes named in the nineteenth century after the notable Judge Ara Spence. The Judge lived nearby at, of course, Spence's Landing, which some years later would be renamed Snow Hill Landing, finally to become Public Landing. The Public Landing of today bears only a slight resemblance to the bayside community in the Judge's time; although, arriving now at the end of Public Landing Road, the first view of the Chincoteague Bay with Assateague Island looming on the horizon can be magical... a timeless vista across water.

Public Landing is historically notable as the first recreation center and vacation destination on the seaside. Before Ocean City became the principal watering hole in Worcester County, Public Landing was the main drawing card, with its hotel and rooming facilities, bathhouse, boat docks, and an impressive pier with a covered pavilion for music, dancing, and carnival attractions. It was, in those early days, all that one might now nostalgically imagine, in sepia tones, of a Victorian playground for the local farmers and villagers: a well-dressed public, with straw hats, starched dresses, and cover-all black bathing suits. For many years, Public Landing hosted Farmer's Day, one of the great summer events on the seaside. Crowds of people drawn from all over the Lower Eastern Shore would arrive on the first Thursday of August, by wagon and carriage, bringing with them hampers of country cooking, smoked hams and beaten biscuits, and cream-infused desserts that could produce an epidemic of diabetes among a less immune population.

Today Public Landing, though still quite charming, is scaled down considerably from its glory days. The 1933 Hurricane destroyed the grand old pier, and while a smaller version was rebuilt later, it would never recover its role as a recreation center. DeGuilbert's, a rococo-embellished hotel in the nineteenth century style, burned to the ground in 1973; although the Mansion House, a B&B currently situated strategically at water-side, is still a fine resting place. That this small settlement has recently become a target for potential large-scale development and expansion into the surrounding crop lands is, however, reason for some concern—an initial crack in the barrier against creeping urbanism from the north.

Taylor Landing, a few miles south of Public Landing and abreast of the small village of Girdletree, is another step back in time—a prize waiting to be discovered by the various factions. Once busy with commercial oystering, Taylor Landing has been virtually deserted much of the year for over a generation. In another, more prosperous time, Taylor Landing was known as Onley's Landing. This earlier boom time has all but vanished from the memories of even local octogenarians. The hazy history of bustling commerce in the first half of the twentieth century is nonetheless revealing about the ensuing changes in bay ecology from natural causes as well as from waterfront growth and development.

The following report is taken from a dispatch to the *Sun* from Ocean City in 1901, filed by a member of the *Sun* staff while on a visit to Worcester County. Apparently Mr. Onley, from whom the landing then took its name, was enjoying the heyday of his enormously successful oyster farming operation:

> "At Onley's the oyster product is yearly from 22,000 to 30,000 barrels of the finest oysters that grow. The price realized at the landing is $2.50 to $3 a barrel without passing through the hands of commission agents, and all of it sold direct to New York...The conditions for growth are quite as favorable as in any part of the

Chesapeake...There is the additional advantage that the Worcester planters, though working individually, protect and respect each other's rights. One reason for this is that they are all planters and have no public (oyster) bars to squabble over and lure them from the practice of regulated industry. There is no oyster police or fishery force...Every planter has his grounds staked off, and there is no more invasion of the oyster plantation than there is of cornfields on land. There is every condition to promote and stimulate the industry, and happy would it be for the whole State if the same conditions could exist elsewhere.

"In a snug little harbor were moored a number of bugeyes, schooners and other craft used by the planters. Mr. Onley has a gasoline launch and some houseboats for the varied purposes of business and pleasure. The houseboats are fitted up for living comfortably on board by fishermen...Many fishermen in Worcester live the whole year in these ark-like structures, which are moved from place to place to meet the requirements of the season.

"...Near Onley's Landing are several islands, some of them high ground, with good cultivatable land. Among these is notably Mill's Island, which was formerly a prime rendezvous for the aborigines. On this island many interesting remains of the Indians are constantly found near the shell piles which the original possessors have left to indicate that they too were fond of oysters. Stone implements, including axes, arrow heads, hollowed stones used for grinding cereals and even pottery have been found in quantities on this spot. Mr. Onley says he has often found skulls and skeletons of Indians which have been washed out of their burial places."

The glory days of oystering soon ended. The oysters began to die from disease, natural predators, and changes in water quality resulting from the closure of inlets on Assateague Island. By the time of the Great Depression, the harvest yield and prices had dropped to unsupportable levels. A generation after the closure of Onley's operation, an attempt was made to revive the industry. But this time the transplanting of oysters from the Chesapeake Bay was limited to a short bath—just long enough to rinse away the Chesapeake Bay blandness and gain the zesty, salty tang of the coastal bays—but not long enough to be exposed to the lethal viruses, oyster bores, and worms that would otherwise take their toll. After a few changes of tide to "salt up," these brief visitors to the coastal bays were labeled as Chincoteague oysters, and the price marked up substantially based on the fame of the seaside oysters having a much superior taste. This operation, too, would fold. Only the oyster shells packed into the driveway and scattered around the old shacks serve as a reminder of this formerly bustling operation.

Current efforts to re-establish "wild" oysters in the coastal bays, spearheaded by the Assateague Coastal Trust, may have a better ending—adding back a significant element of biodiversity, if not a lucrative commercial opportunity.

In the meantime, Taylor Landing remains a good spot to launch a boat and spend a day of recreation on lightly-traveled water trails. From the public boat ramp, the view across Johnson Bay, an indentation within the Chincoteague Bay, sweeps over privately-owned islands, such as Tizzards, Assacorkin and Mills Islands—highly coveted as sportsmen's retreats. Assacorkin, in the ancient Algonquian language, may be translated as "where there is yellow land beyond," with the "beyond" presumably referring to Assateague Island, a few miles eastward over the broader bay. Here, in the lee of these islands and in the small coves and tributaries are excellent destinations for shallow-drafted craft. A guide map for paddlers, included here, shows the most accessible water trails just to the south of Taylor Landing. An equally enticing water trail lies to the north and enters Box Iron Creek just south of Rattlesnake Island. The tidewater scene here is little changed from the days when Box Iron Indians, of the Assateague tribe, settled along the banks.

But be careful. The benign-looking Chincoteague Bay, and even the smaller subsidiary coves, can be treacherous in rough weather. Boaters have drowned here in water no more than chest-deep. When the wind is up, the smaller craft, paddlers especially, should stick to the sheltered sloughs and creeks.

Immediately to the south of Taylor Landing is one of the least-appreciated natural attractions of the lower coastal bays, the E. A. Vaughn Wildlife Management Area.

EAVWMA comprises 2,360 acres of oak and pine forests, scrub brush, fields planted for wildlife, water impoundments, and tidal marshes, which hold a representative assortment of the wildlife of the entire coastal bays watershed. EAVWMA fronts on Johnson Bay and its companion Parker Bay and extends westward to Rt. 12 and south to George Island Landing Road. With several miles of winding shoreline and small navigable guts abundant with fish and fowl, this public land offers the gamut of recreational opportunities—boating, fishing, and crabbing by the shoreline, hiking and birdwatching through extensive nature trails, all-terrain bicycling, and primitive camping. Since the greater portion of EAVWMA is open to public hunting in season, hikers are advised to wander carefully at this time, or to stay within the refuge area in the northeastern portion that is accessible from Taylor Landing Road.

The conservation values of EAVWMA are now being extended over thousands of surrounding acres through the designation of this section of the county as a federal and state-recognized Rural Legacy Area, a voluntary program for saving open space and historic sites. Conservation easements have been put in place on a number of contiguous farm lands, whereby the owners are compensated for maintaining the undeveloped character of their properties in perpetuity. This is a worthy complement to the Assateague Island parks and Chincoteague wildlife refuge—an exceptional chunk of sustainable geography.

Following Taylor Landing Road out to Rt. 12, the next stop is Girdletree—once a part of Fleaville and later taking its name from Girdle Tree Farm that covered much of the settlement. The up-and-down history along this byway is repeated. By the end of the nineteenth century Girdletree was a thriving village, with three churches, two stores, a school, doctor, and post office. At the beginning of the twentieth century, Scarborough's Store advertised itself as the biggest general merchandising center south of Wilmington. As the village continued to grow, it included a bank, two canneries, a stave and barrel factory, hotel, forge, and livery stable. Now, virtually all are gone: the bank closed in '33 with the Great Depression, and other commercial operations were soon to follow. Until a generation ago, a small country general store remained to serve the community: a cooler with milk, eggs, and a few cold cuts; a shelf of canned staples; and a counter spread with work gloves and the like. The glass store-front windows now shed little light on the dark, empty interior. Nevertheless, a smoldering cinder of activity may still be detected in Girdletree—an attractive antique shop and signs of recently vacant, but still-sturdy older homes taking on fresh coats of paint and awaiting new owners.

Girdletree Historical Society (TP: 2004)
Shirley Brown, Clarence Pilchard, Sandra Hudson

(Shirley Brown): Dad and Uncle Milton had Popeye's Clam House at Taylor's Landing. Take on clams or oysters depending on the season. Take 'em up by truck to Philadelphia, Allentown, and to Fulton Fish Market in New York. Started in the thirties, but still doing it in the fifties when we (Shirley and Clarence, sister and brother) grew up. The rest of the year Dad would deliver coal around. We worked the bay with Dad, too. The oysters were big then; our natural oysters, not the ones they later brought over from the Chesapeake just to salt up—they were little bitty things. Ours were big. When you had a single-fry then, you *had* a single-fry, not these little things.

I remember Dad going out and hand-tongin' oysters. He'd put newspapers in his boots to keep his feet warm 'cause they didn't have insulation in them. When we started crabbin', in the early fifties is about the time when crab pots came in. My grandfather, he was still trotlinin'. Clammin'? Most of the time we raked them. Dad would take a bunch of men on his boat, ten or fifteen of them, which was normal, and we would go with them. The men used the clam rakes in the deeper water. We gals went in the shallow water with an inner tube with a burlap bag hung inside or a big, galvanized wash tub tied around our waist, and we would put our clams in that. We dug the clams with our feet. We wore moccasins for that. Then we'd go back to the boat and get some dry clothes on. Open some clams for the sharks that would be gatherin' 'round.

(Clarence Pilchard): The sharks would come right up to you when you were clammin' and you had to push them out of the way. Some of 'em were right big. I remember Charles Richardson use to clam by hisself out around the tumps and there was this big ol' shark used to follow him. We would say to Charlie, here comes your friend. One day Charlie got tired of it and slammed the rake into the side of the shark, and the shark took off and pulled Charlie, who was holding on to the handle, right up out of the water like he was on water skis. We yelled to him, "Let go, let go," so he finally lets go and the shark goes up on a sand bar, flipped over and tore the rake outta his back. But he didn't come around and bother no more.

Most every Sunday morning we'd shuck 5,000 clams, I remember that. Everybody'd sit around the clam house, shuckin' off a big pile of clams. We'd put them in five-gallon containers. You had to be careful not to burst their water sack, because if you busted that you couldn't ship 'em 'cause you had to have a full clam. Pack 'em in big barrels with ice and Dad would truck 'em up to Wilmington, Allentown, Reading, and on the way back down he'd pick up a load of coal.

(Shirley Brown): When did Franklin City die? I'd say after the '33 storm it started. Then the Naval (Air Station) Base closed down at Chincoteague in the late fifties and that was pretty much it. There was a hotel and restaurant still there—Markland's, right down there on the end where they would turn the trains around to head back up to Stockton and Snow Hill and on up. After the base closed, Markland's had to shut down because they had beer and that kind of stuff downstairs and that had attracted the sailors from the base.

Back then, we'd take the boat from Taylor's Landing down to Franklin City. Grandpop wasn't supposed to drink, so Mom would say don't drink any beer...and of course Grandpop would drink too much at Markland's. Comin' back we would hug the marsh and Grandpop would say, "If anything happens, you kids jump off and get up on the marsh."

(Clarence Pilchard): I went down there a couple of weeks ago, and there weren't much left, a couple of houses is all. Storms, weather, nobody took care of things. And the railroad's long gone. It's a shame they tore up all those tracks. It would have been interestin' for people today, you know, tourists and the like, to make that trip down the line to Franklin City and back.

(Sandra Hudson, Shirley Brown, and Clarence Pilchard, alternately): Especially when we had company, everybody went down to the bay, the women in their coats and hats. And we had pictures of the men holding the oysters up like this, you know, like they're ready to slurp them down. For as long as (I) can possibly remember, we always rode to the bay. Mother and Daddy still rode to the bay. We still do that. Before we go anywhere, we ride to the bay.

What would we like to see happen here? We'd like to see a little more than what is happening! All agreed? Put us back the way it was in the early fifties. The boys were busy, we had stores. Now you can't survive. Like Grandpop's seafood bar...you couldn't do it anyway, the seafood's just not here and the county might not let you put up what you would want to anyway. Then, you didn't have to go nowhere. It was all right here. Yeah, hotel, the cannery which employed lots of people... shoe store, barbershop...and the hat shop, the Redmen Hall. And we had the school, bank...and there was our general store and groceries. We had Barnes's, which was the biggest general merchandise store anywhere around. It's gone now; stood where the fire house is now, where our Church Hall was at one time. It was a wonderful building. We didn't have to go to big stores unless we took a trip up to Pennsylvania.

When my son (Shirley Brown's) came home from the first Persian Gulf War, he wanted to open a mini-market but the county wouldn't let him, because he wouldn't

have enough parking places. I mean, come on, not enough parking places in Girdletree? He's out in Montana now.

Just a few miles down Rt. 12 is Stockton, once known as Ticktown and later as Stock Town, a bustling livestock center and rail switch. In its frontier days Stock Town was a round-up point for cattle, which would be driven to city markets along a seaside version of the Chisholm Trail. Like Girdletree, Stock Town boasted an impressive group of commercial enterprises—canneries, seafood packing houses, lumber yard, general stores and a bank. For the present, all is gone, even the former name. The village population of latter-day Stockton has been shrinking for years. As in other settlements along the Chincoteague Bay, once-attractive older homes are begging for new owners who are looking for a tranquil get-away or an affordable fixer-upper. Fine brick commercial buildings, now empty, command the village's one crossroads. Still, there is a charm that remains. No traffic noise, and the price is right.

Turning left in Stockton, at the crossroads onto George Island Landing Road, the trail dead-ends at yet another public landing that has seen better times. Its decay is also the stuff of picturesque photographs, though the signs of a commercial fishing economy gone awry are unsettling here as elsewhere.

The journey along Maryland's coastal bays might stop here, a one-way trip of about thirty-five miles from Berlin, including a few short detours down dead-end roads that lead into sprawling bayside farms and privately owned boat landings. However, it's only another ten miles or so on to Chincoteague Island in Virginia and the south end of Assateague Island, and it's well worth pushing on. The Virginia portion along the coastal bays is a part of the whole, has much to offer the visitor, and adds to a perspective of the watershed.

Following the back road out of George Island Landing, a few minutes' drive leads to the next village, Greenbackville, situated just over the Maryland-Virginia line. Greenbackville, or just Greenback, is livelier than the previous stops. On the waterfront, boat slips are filled with crabbers, clammers, and gill netters, as well as a number of private pleasure craft.

Fishermen are sorting out and repairing their nets, crabbers unloading the day's catch, and the trucks of wholesale seafood operators moving in and out. Greenback's popularity among commercial watermen is not unlike that of a roadhouse saloon that straddles state lines and shuffles customers in the front and out the back door to take advantage of the prevailing Blue Laws in each state. Fishing regulations that vary from state to state can cause much the same thing.

Before heading on, there may be time to stop at the fish house restaurant by the docks. The oysters on the half-shell are salty and absolutely fresh. Fish and crabs are right off the watermen's boats. Why hurry?

Just below Greenback, an even busier seafood trade once flourished at Franklin City, the end of the railroad line that reached through Stockton and Basket Switch all the way back to the city markets of Philadelphia and beyond. The train would take on the catch from the Chincoteague fisherman, providing the island community its main source of revenues for over half a century. Then the railroad folded and so did Franklin City, but not the village of Chincoteague.

The history and development of Chincoteague Island, along with the former settlement at Assateague Point on the barrier island, parallel in many ways that of the Maryland seaside. Old native families have moved back and forth across the state line for generations. There is a sharing of a similar heritage. However, one difference is that Chincoteague Island is a half-step or so behind its neighbors to the north, appearing somewhat like the Ocean City of fifty years ago. Visitors will know when they are in native Teaguer territory upon hearing their peculiar rhythm of speech, similar to, but more pronounced than, the now rarely encountered native dialect over the Maryland line. The ancient speech patterns have been partially preserved by a longer period of isolation of the island residents. Until the causeway to Chincoteague Island was built to link with the mainland in 1963, it was not uncommon to run across a Teaguer who had never been off the island in an entire lifetime: "Why should I? Ain't nothin' over there I need." Tough people. Nevertheless, the leap forward is on the horizon, as the newer resident population of "Come Heres" are catching up in numbers with the native Teaguers. Worcester Count passed that stage some time ago.

Vacationers and day-visitors, drawn by the bathing beaches and nature trails of Assateague Island and the resort life of Chincoteague, now underpin the local economy. Although the high season is summer, there is a year-around tourist business, in large part fostered by visitors coming to watch the constant coming and going of migratory water birds in the wildlife refuge.

Today, the biggest single event in Chincoteague is Pony Penning, the local fair that runs each year in July for the benefit of the Chincoteague Volunteer Fire Department. (The term "pony" will undoubtedly endure in Chincoteague, though the equine status is being elevated to "horse" on the Maryland portion of the island.) Pony Penning began nearly a century ago with the auctioning of the Assateague ponies as a low-key fund-raiser. Early on, the ponies brought ten to fifteen dollars a head. After World War II, a pony might bring as much as a hundred dollars, as attendance grew and the weekend fair blossomed into a main event with major media coverage. In July 2001, thousands were on hand as one pony brought the extraordinary record price of $10,500.

Times were changing even in Chincoteague.

Biking the Coastal Bays

Coastal biking excursions are linked with 2,500 miles of historic rural byways published as "Great Delmarva Biking Trails."

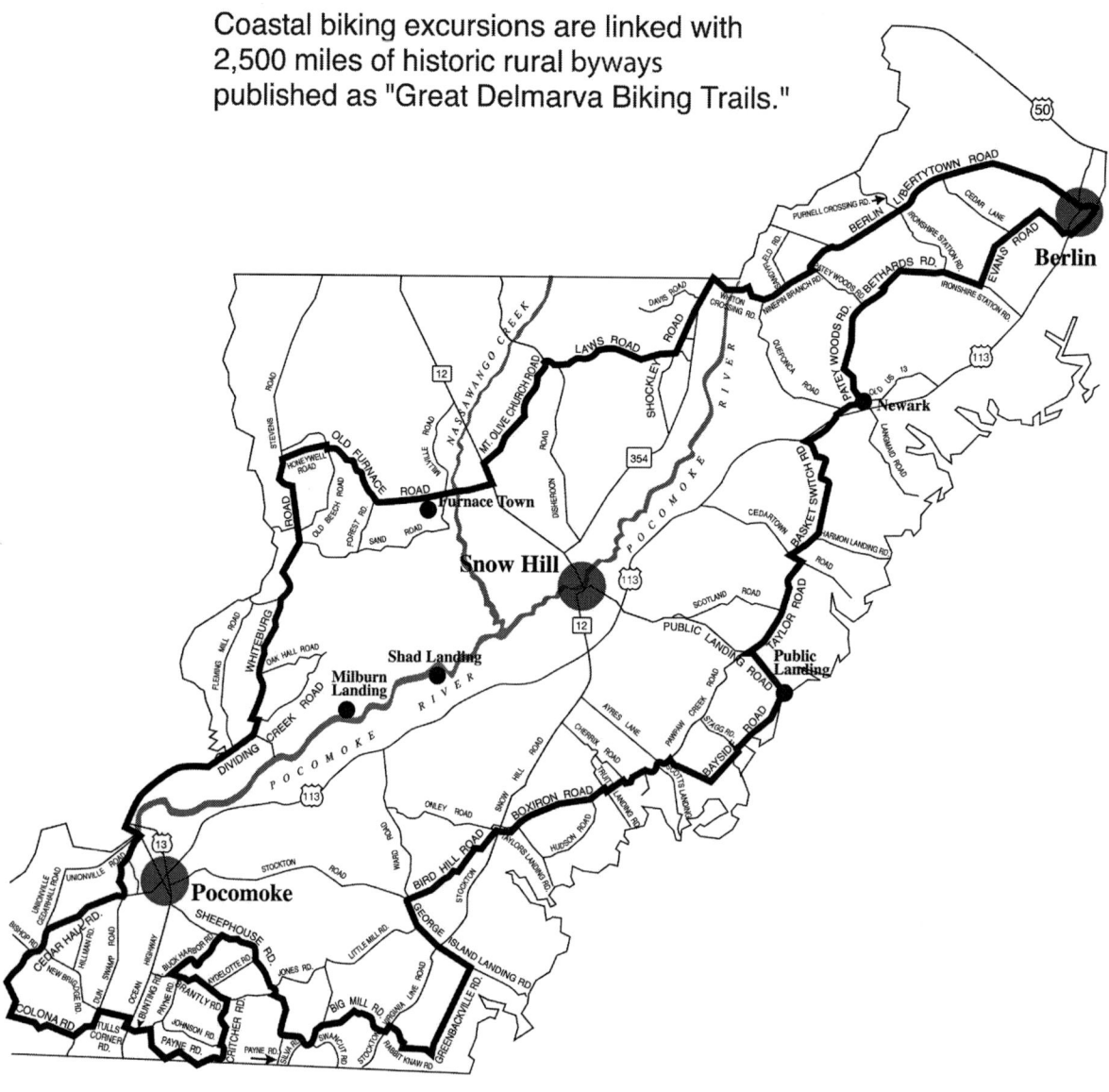

Public Landing

Vacationers and day-trippers would gather on the Fourth of July and throughout the summer to enjoy the attractions by the Chincoteague Bay: going to the movies and dancing in the ballroom located on the pier; picnicking in the park; treating the children to cotton candy and candied apples; or renting a boat for an outing on the water. Then came the 1933 Hurricane. Much of Public Landing was demolished. A scaled-down pier was reconstructed too late to bring back the crowds. Public Landing had lost its momentum, as attention now turned to the newer resort of Ocean City. Nevertheless, Public Landing still exudes a quiet charm.

Photos courtesy of Julia A. Purnell Museum

Girdletree and Stockton: Agricultural Legacies

Packing Apples for the Market, Early 20th Century (left)

Until after World War II, berry-raising farms along the lower coastal bays made Worcester County the strawberry capital of Delmarva. Harrison's peach orchards were promoted as the most extensive in the entire country. Tomatoes, cucumbers, and potatoes drew hundreds of migrant workers at harvest time. The canning factories hummed. Then, in the space of a very few years, the truck farms and fruit orchards were turned into soy bean and cornfields and the canning factories closed.

Truck Farming, Early 20th Century (below)

Photos courtesy of Julia A. Purnell Museum

Watermen at Onley's Landing, circa 1910

In the days when oysters thrived in the coastal bays.

Photo courtesy of Julia A. Purnell Museum

Heritage Preservation and Neglect, Side-by-Side

Girdletree Bank: example of what can be done.

Girdletree General Store: example of the extensive graveyard of once-occupied commercial buildings and residences.

Photos by the author

Chincoteague Pony Penning

Ponies are being driven across the narrow channel that separates Assateague Island from the island-town of Chincoteague—on their way to the auction block.

Photo courtesy of National Park Service

Coastal Bays Kayak Trails

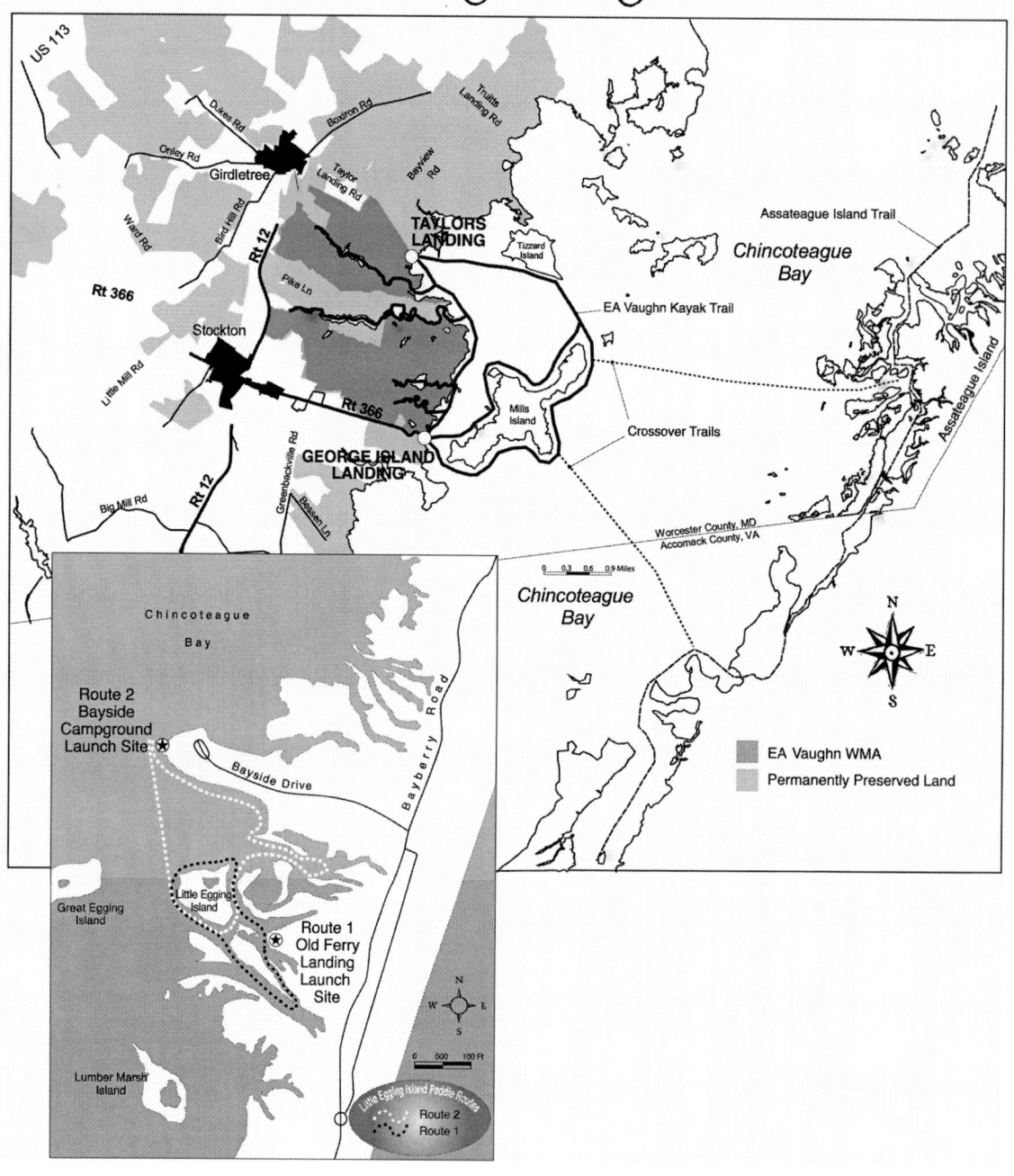

XII

A change of clothes the black-bellied plovers know,
blends in with the ice and snow,
and the goldfinch tones down to grey and brown;
then the birder knows, too, it's not just the only,
it's the best game around.

Birding Adventures

The geography of Maryland's coastal bays offers a complete recipe to attract a diversity of bird life, hardly matched elsewhere in the United States. The watershed contains magnetic peninsulas, large blocks of contiguous forest lands, marshy points, scrubby hammocks, and the elongated attraction of Assateague Island. And all this is encased within the more expansive Delmarva Peninsula, which taken together act as a natural toll gate and resting place on the migratory highway.

Added to this favorable shape of land masses, there is water everywhere, with each body and size and chemical composition, from freshwater ponds and brackish creeks to the salty bays and ocean. More than 360 species can be regularly counted from among the shorebirds, waterfowl, raptors, song birds, and upland game birds. The seasonal passage is often spectacular. That the United Nations has recognized the watershed as an "internationally significant" migratory bird corridor is well deserved.

Once a minor pastime on the seaside—the birder considered a strange bird indeed by local residents—birdwatching has become a significant component of the tourism dollar, with millions being pumped annually into the economy by nature lovers outfitted with their field glasses. It's a pastime that knows no seasons, requires little paraphernalia, and can be done in a number of different settings without bumping into a competitive army of other outdoor enthusiasts.

Ilia Fehrer (NPS: 2004)

The north end of Assateague is one of the best nesting areas for piping plover, which are an endangered species. A lot of people, of course, don't know about piping plovers and the poor little piping plovers are well camouflaged. Their eggs are extremely well camouflaged, and they lay their eggs in between a couple of little stones. You can walk over them and walk right on one those eggs, and you wouldn't know it until after you picked up your foot and you had a mess on your foot. It is a job for the park service—the rangers who have to monitor it—to protect that nesting habitat. They've put in enclosure areas where they know there are nesting areas—to keep people away and to (help protect against) marauding birds, the seagulls. Another problem for the piping plover are the foxes.

However, if the bird watcher prefers company or to be involved in organized outings, there is much to offer here, as well. The Delmarva Birding Weekend each April is timed with the migration of neotropical song birds, shorebirds, and waders. Trips afield may combine boating and bike rides, as well as detours through the area's historic sites. Within a short drive from Maryland's coastal bays, other birding events occur during the year. To name only a few: the International Migratory Bird Celebration on the Eastern Shore of Virginia in

May; the Eastern Shore Birding Festival in October, from Chincoteague to Kiptopeake, Virginia; Waterfowl Week in Chincoteague around the Thanksgiving weekend; and annual Christmas Bird Counts held throughout the area, with one traditional event focused around the Isle of Wight and Sinepuxent Bays. The most promising new highlight is a Cape to Cape Birding Trail—from Cape May, New Jersey, to Cape Charles-Kiptopeake, Virginia. The lead organizer is Delmarva LITE, which is also helping package other nature-based pursuits, including Delmarva biking and canoe and kayak trails.

Several more personal birdwatching experiences that come to mind start at the lower end of the coastal bays, at the Chincoteague National Wildlife Refuge, the birding jewel in the seaside crown. Ironically, a primary reason for establishing the wildlife refuge in 1943 was to protect the endangered snow geese, a goal that has been overly achieved. The population of the geese has rebounded dramatically, and in the fall and winter the many thousands of snow geese often blanket the water impoundments (officially designated as "wet soil management areas") and overflow into the coastal bays and farm lands throughout the Delmarva Peninsula. Acres of farm crops and marsh grasses can be wiped out in a single day's feeding. This, in turn, leads to soil erosion and loss of beneficial habitat for other wildlife. Nevertheless, the spectacular view of wildlife in a splendid setting, surrounded by the ocean and bay, is partial compensation.

Wintering ducks, brant, and both Canada and snow geese begin to arrive in early fall and peak in late winter, just before the grand "staging" for their northward journey to the nesting grounds. Their loss is followed by fresh migrations of waders and songbirds. So it goes through the seasons.

While most of the attention in the refuge is given to water birds, the songbirds, though less visible in their shrubby and wooded habitats, are worth pursuing on foot. Good birding trails branch away from Wildlife Loop, the vehicular passage encircling the water impoundments. Considerable data have been collected on the song birds by Dick Roberts, a retired analytical chemist. Roberts has been carrying out a multi-year banding program on contract with the wildlife refuge and with the sponsorship of the Assateague Coastal Trust.

Setting light, small-meshed "mist" nets, Roberts captures and bands annually up to 1,000 birds from some 250 different species. His reports are added to those from other banding stations in the region, establishing solid information on migratory patterns and populations. The accumulated data are then published annually in *North American Bird Bander*. Incidentally, volunteers are welcome to help in the banding program.

A recent trip to the wildlife refuge late in August found the impoundments turned to hard-baked mud flats, caused by months of severe drought and the intentional lowering of water levels to allow regrowth of vegetation for the migratory waders and dabblers. While not the best time to see the widest variety of species, a long-awaited thunderstorm had just passed over and a small herd of Chincoteague ponies, loosed from their normal enclosure and were finding patches of marsh hay to their liking. Cattle egrets were picking at the ponies' droppings. Sika moved quietly by the thickets bordering the parched mud flat. Several blue herons and a green heron stood motionless in the ditch by the road. There, for a moment, the scene could be any other savanna in the natural world—substituting only the ponies and the sika for the ungulates of other lands. It's hard to come away disappointed with a trip to the Chincoteague National Wildlife Refuge.

Another kind of birding is to be had in the search for classic wooden decoys, fashioned by legendary carvers whose pieces adorn museums and private collections throughout the country. Chincoteague Bay has been a home to this art form that started out as a simple craft—making a rig of "stools" for fellow gunners to knock about with during the season. When factories took over the business of mass-producing cheaper and easier-to-handle plastic decoys, one might have thought the days of the nicked-up old wooden blocks were over. Instead, the fifty-cent stool of earlier days increased astronomically in value, especially if the provenance could be traced to an Ira Hudson, Miles Hancock, Doug Jester, or "Cigar" Daisey. A rare specimen with original paint intact has brought well over a quarter-million dollars at auction.

The upper bays have produced their own carvers, if not generally on the same level. A few collectable "primitives" are still around that may be traced back to Capt. John Smith, who gunned the Sinepuxent Bay for the better part of his 100 years. Bennett Scott, a current world-class specialist in the derivative form of decorative-bird carving, has few peers in this enormously competitive field. His nature ensembles of various species of birds are etched to the last feather, blade of grass, or perching branch.

Before the collecting of working decoys and decorative bird carvings evolved into the big-money business and hobby of today, the amateur collector might happen upon an Ira Hudson or Miles Hancock in the corner of an antique shop, or hear of some elderly widow who was selling off her late husband's decoys and old shotguns stored in the attic. Eyes brighten at the very thought. Not very likely anymore, though just the glimmer of a rare find still makes the search interesting.

Another Kind of Birding
Miles Hancock (NPS: 1971)

So I said to myself, "I'll try my luck on 'em," (making duck decoys). So I commenced makin' the heads. Then I commenced making the bodies. Ira (Hudson) and myself, we'd go down to Guildford and buy a truckload of blocks. Well, the first dozen that I sold, I sold to Ira and he painted 'em up as baldcrowns, (though) I made 'em for bluebills. And that's what started me off. Course I've had a good life. I been out in the bay when no other boat ever showed itself.

I got so when I had the heart attack—it was bad—I had to give up makin' large decoys and I started these little miniatures here....find that people wanted 'em so bad, I said I think I can make a go, which I have. There was such a demand that I couldn't keep into 'em. But it's getting greater here all the time with tourists—more people, more people. And where people has had my pictures in papers and books and so forth, why they got to look me up so they can get a souvenir. And when I was in the movies, that started me off.... With the small ones and all with what I got on hand, I've made somewheres around forty thousand—to my best knowledge.

They're not many black ducks as there was...because the trappers got so numerous they almost broke 'em up. But there's quite a few raises on the beach. Course, broadbills and redheads has left us in that '33 storm. We had 'em here by thousands, I guess might would say millions; but it took all the feed out of the bay, what we call eel grass. Now our ducks goes on the west coast line. Well, way back there, the old shelduck would come down in October and these broadbills. But later the redheads would come in and the brant and the geese. But in freezes, when the bays just froze up north, I've seen black ducks comin' from Jersey. We call 'em Jersey ducks. They had red feet, big yella beaks. I've seen 'em fly fer two days, jus' bunch after bunch, and you could look anywheres and the sky were a bunch of black ducks jus' goin' south...and they'd come down below Franklin City, down in der restin' place 'til night, ya see, then they come back to the flats. And den of a mornin', when they flirt up, they'd come up between the shoals and the mainland...there were just bunch after bunch, they wasn't all together, but strung out like that. That bunch would be outta your sight and dey still comin' in. Now, nobody won't believe that today, but that's de real fact.

Delbert "Cigar" Daisey (NPS: 1971)

The first decoy that I ever made and painted for myself or replaced heads or somethin' like that would be around 1940. Just make one once in a while...'course since then I've made, oh, about five, six thousand pieces, I 'spect.

Well, when I first started making decoys, I actually never had no saws or nothin' like that. I jus' used an old hatchet, sharpened it up real sharp and chop 'em out with this ol' hatchet and with a pocket knife. And a piece of rough sandpaper. We'd leave 'em pretty rough 'cause they hold paint good.

I'll go to a chopping block and start on somethin' and won't draw nothin'. If it turns out good why it turns out good. If it don't, I turn it into somethin' else. If it's a big

> one, I'll make a little one out of it....Ya ain't gonna make no money out of it to start with, 'cause there's no money in it. It's jus', what do you call it, a labor of love.
>
> Seven days is not enough days in the week for you; you can work all of 'em, if you want to and you still don't see where you've done nothin'. And the better the grade you make, naturally the less pieces you make during the year. Then that puts the price up so that you sorta thin the buyers out.
>
> I can work a week on a good black duck—well, as good a black duck as I can make, I'll put it that way. From the day I walk to the bandsaw, saw him out, 'til the last feather's painted on 'im, put a keel on 'im, ready to go to a show...you can figure a full week in that bird. I always liked the black duck. He's a duck of this vicinity. He's smart. I like the looks of 'im, too: 'ol big bay drake with a right light face, you know, yellowish bill, high chrome-yellow bill. I always leaned toward 'im.
>
> Another problem you run into, people find ya. Fer instance last Saturday I had thirty-four people some see me—well, if they didn't come see me, I couldn't sell nothin'. But on the other hand, you can figure twenty minutes a piece for 'em and, well, your day is gone and you ain't got nothin' done.

In January, a plunge in temperature will often freeze the refuge impoundments, sending many of the water birds out to look for food and open water. Many flee farther south. Others move north up the coastal bays in search of ice-free bays and bare sand bars. Extraordinary concentrations of water birds begin to form in the upper coastal bays, from the Verrazano Bridge to the Delaware line, where the swifter tidal currents flowing in and out of the Ocean City Inlet maintain a ribbon of open water.

It is now the middle of a recent January and the deep cold has set in. Ordinary humans might prefer to hunker down on the couch and watch the Super Bowl; but they would be missing a waterfowl spectacle that is the equivalent of a once-in-a-lifetime meteor shower for stargazers. Every imaginable wintering water bird in the Atlantic flyway is concentrated among the ice floes along a several-mile stretch, perhaps no more than a hundred yards wide, now just holding on until the weather breaks. The bays are eerily quiet, except for the chatter of the fowl. A snowy harbor seal is taking refuge on a marsh bank by Snug Harbor, a solitary wanderer from among the wintry ocean currents. The blustery arctic weather is inhospitable even to the dogged clam-dredging watermen.

Best views of this winter display are at the Verrazano Bridge and around the Ocean City Inlet and Rt. 50 Bridge. The very hardy birder can walk up North Beach and across to the bay-side of the island, or the truly arctic-insulated enthusiast may launch a light craft from wherever a shoreline opening in the ice permits. Out on the bays in these conditions is truly out of this world.

Then, as the ice begins to break up, with the wind coming around from the northwest to a southerly direction, another opportunity has come along. The extremely low spring (lunar) tides appear on the full and new moons. Water has retreated from the shoreline and appears to have been sucked into a great underground reservoir. Sand bars and mud flats, replacing much of the watery basin, are crawling with worms and snails and other edibles, on which the "peeps" and other shorebirds have gathered in darting flocks to be first in line to gourmandize on the winter banquet table. It's a joy to watch. This is a good time, too, for the bird watchers to wander over the sand bars and "sign" a few clams to take home and enjoy their own late-winter feast.

Another winter visit brings us back to the E. A. Vaughn Wildlife Management Area, the fine birding spot located along the coastal bays between Girdletree and Stockton. The EAVWMA website describes it thus: "Woodcock, hairy and downy woodpeckers, and warblers inhabit the extensive forest. In the marshes, great blue herons, geese and little blue herons, as well as common and snow egrets hunt for fish. Black ducks, mallards, Canada and snow geese, and other waterfowl use the marshes and open water found in and around the area. Wood ducks are especially attracted to an area of forest deliberately flooded in the fall when the trees are dormant. This area is called a 'greentree reservoir' and is also home to frogs and toads, turtles and snakes. Endangered Delmarva fox squirrels were released in the area and have been thriving there for a decade. Because of their preference for open woodlands and wood edges, these squirrels are often observed from cars driving along the woods. Migrating hawks can be seen in the fall as they travel down the coast."

As we enter EAVWMA from Taylor Landing Road on this chilling morning, the sun reflects brightly on the refuge ponds casting a lovely light, moving shadows over wavering reeds; the air is salty. Surprisingly, there are no ducks at the moment in the water-management area, although blue herons and great white egrets are working the shallows. A bald eagle flies by, then a northern harrier, or marsh hawk. It is to be a morning of hawk sightings, and giving thought to the practical vernacular names bestowed on them by country people: a red-tailed hawk (chicken hawk), merlin (pigeon hawk), and an American kestrel (sparrow hawk). Farther, on a wooded trail lined with red oaks, the forest floor is covered with a bountiful mast crop. No wild turkeys are in sight, but just off the trail are fresh scratchings—sure signs that a flock passed by earlier in the morning.

Driving around the perimeter of EAVWMA, we nose into an entrance on George Island Landing Road. Several bird hunters, parked at the pull-in, appear to be finishing up a morning's shoot. They are well-attired, with nice guns and a fine-looking bird dog. Probably not local is the immediate impression.

Curious, we ask, "Any luck?"

"We jumped seven woodcock. Got one. That's about our average. By the way, are there any quail around here? We didn't run across any."

"Used to be, but hasn't been much quail shooting in years. It seems like they're disappearing around here. You used to find a covey in every little piece of cover, but not any more. Something's going on, it seems."

"Must be. We're finding the same thing everywhere we go. Anyway, this is a fabulous place, just walking through it." The one hunter pauses, and then asks politely, "And what are you doing around here?"

"Just progging." This evokes the squint of a silent query. "Oh, checking out a few things for some writing about the coastal bays."

"Really? That's great. This place around here sure deserves it."

Piping Plover

Endangered species, under protection and holding its own on Assateague Island.

Photo courtesy of National Park Service

Wintering Waterfowl, Sinepuxent Bay

January freeze-up, 2004.

Photo by the author

Birding & Boating the Coastal Bays

1. The Pocomoke River meanders through pristine woodlands
2. Bird the beautiful bald cypress of the Nassawango Creek
3. Search Corker's Creek for flycatchers, green herons & hawks
4. See night birds at the E.A. Vaughn Wildlife Management Area
5. Stroll the meadows for quail, turkeys, indigo buntings & wood ducks
6. Along the "Life of the Dunes Trail" listen for rails & owls
7. Search for egrets, willets and ponies on Assateague Island
8. Tour Assateague Island by boat for a glimpse of varius seabirds
9. See the largest variety of birds in one spot in the Mid-Atlantic

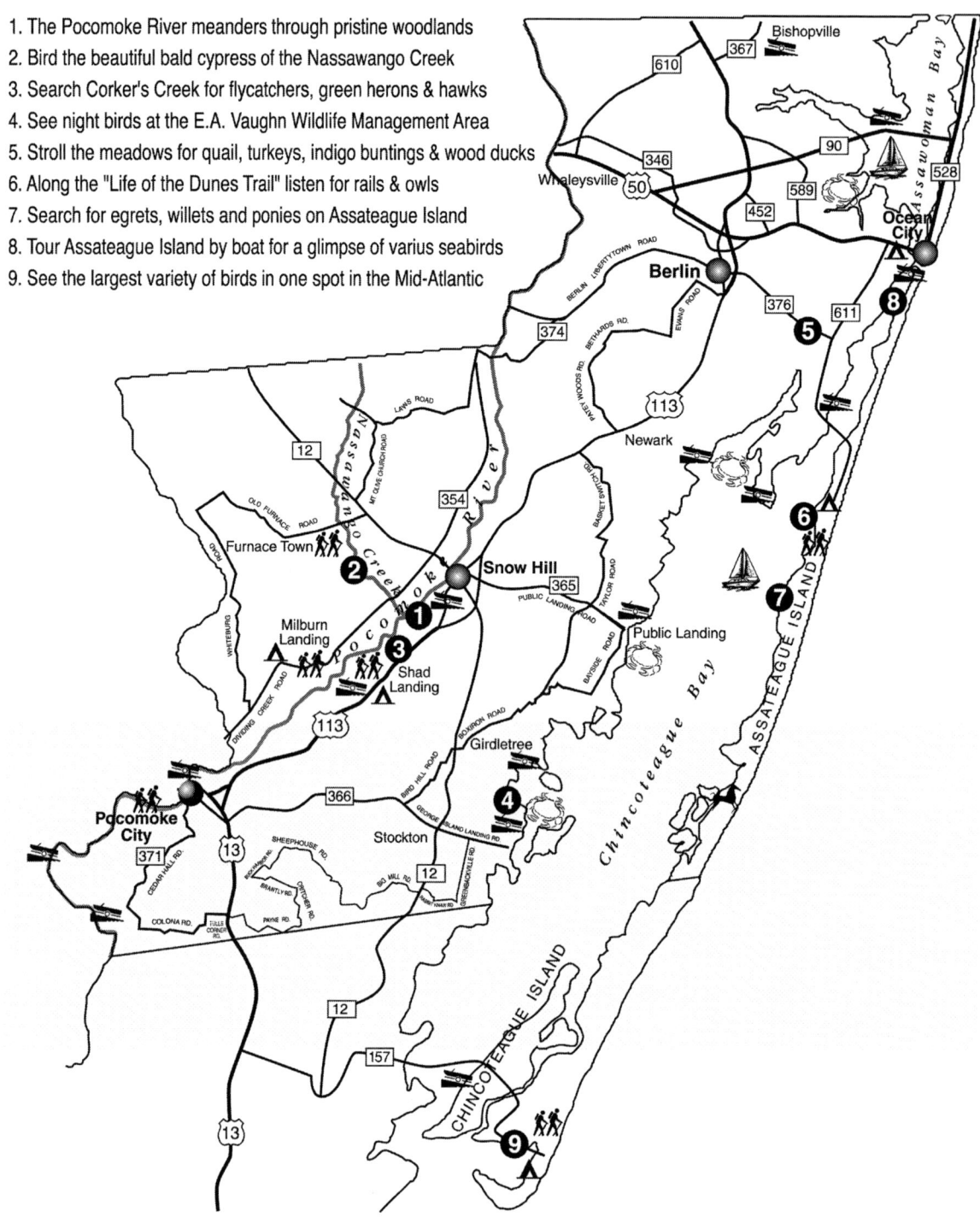

XIII

On the bank of the creek as the day is done,
the great blue heron stands alone,
crook in the neck and hunch in the back,
its beak a spear intent on one last snack;
it's now down the gullet, like a chug of beer.

A Solitary Outing: Reflections by an Elm Tree

A canoe or kayak would do just fine on the serpentine water trail of Trappe Creek, once called Assateague River by English settlers claiming lands along Maryland's coastal bays in the 1600s. The Assateague Indians first plied the creeks and out into the bays in dugouts, which later gave way to the sailing vessels of the European explorers and colonists, then on to motor-powered vessels. Now the trend is back to paddle-power.

A good starting point is at the base of the bridge at Ayres Creek, a tributary of Trappe Creek, located on Assateague Road (Rt. 376) one mile west of Rt. 611. Here lies the borderline between the urban quadrant in northeastern Worcester County and rural country in the southern part of the county. To travel this tributary is to see both worlds.

Paddle either way, but, if time for only one direction, head south towards the mouth of Trappe Creek at Newport Bay. Immediately after departing the bridge (going south), the boater will pass Golden Quarter Farm, dating to 1678. The name Golden Quarter was supposedly derived from a field of wild yellow coreopsis located between the entrance lane and creek, though the glimmering yellow flower might well have been the more prevalent and native black-eyed Susan. The stately home, extensively remodeled in the past few years, was originally constructed in 1770, and occupied shortly thereafter by Major Joshua Prideaux. According to legend, one of the major's ancestors was an immigrant French Huguenot who came ashore from a wrecked ship, afloat on a hencoop, fetching with him little else. Now read Perdue for Prideaux, a subsequent anglicizing of the ancestral French name, and we may have advanced from hencoop to chicken empire, such being the influence of bloodlines.

Much of what is known about the early life at Golden Quarter and the surroundings has been passed along as oral history, or in the odd pieces of local write-ups. Sara Prideaux, a talkative daughter of the Major, has left us accounts of genteel living on the estate in the late eighteenth and early nineteenth centuries. Family life was blissful, though this may be filtered through the memory of one having lived in an affluent household. The major not only grew crops on his self-sustaining plantation, he also managed the property's mill, and owned a country store where he sold whiskey by the gallon. In the rest of his spare time, he hauled seine by night in the tidal shallows of the creek and bay, providing a fresh supply of seafood for the family table. He built ships and sailed them as far as New York, bred Muscovy ducks and fancy cattle, and, as a member of the Council of Maryland, participated in the administrations of church and state. Here, truly, was a merchant-planter.

The remaining trunk of a famous English elm tree, a witness to more than two centuries of the social life, stands nakedly by the driveway at Golden Quarter, just barely in view from the creek. Known as the Ayres Elm, it was ninety feet tall with a girth of just over twenty feet. Its huge size served as a landmark for boatmen coming up the Chincoteague and

Newport Bays. The champion elm died a decade or so ago, possibly from neglect during a period of absentee ownership rather than from the more obvious Dutch elm disease.

Golden Quarter was recently purchased by Mrs. Sandra Frazier, the current resident and avid preserver of the property.

Almost directly across the creek, to the east, is a modern classic—the stark glass house designed and built in the 1990s in the Philip Johnson style for current resident, Dean Jenkins, a local attorney. Over 200 years of change in styles face each other—from the warm and intimate heart pine to the sheer openness of glass structure—both outstanding models of their times. One might think of the glass pyramid erected a few years back in front of the Louvre, which nearly brought on a riot between French traditionalists and modernists. Today, the contrast of glass and old stone along the Seine hardly draws a questioning glance.

Paddle along and reach the confluence of Ayres and Trappe Creeks—the latter being the dominant tributary. Turn right, westward, and Trappe Creek slowly narrows until it completely runs out of steam at the once historic village of Trappe, an ancient gristmill settlement, which has since been replaced by several contemporary homes and an off-and-on-again country store. Here, during the Revolutionary War, Stephen Decatur's parents disembarked by the gristmill on their way to a humble hide-away for the famous birthing event of baby Stephen, who would become the young nation's famous naval hero.

Or continue more or less due south and pass between wide marshes with a background of pine forests, tidewater ponds, and grain fields. Along the western shoreline, especially, are large contiguous farms that retain a centuries-old flavor of the original plantations that not only fed the region but supplied food and lumber supplies to seaports from New York to Norfolk. It is also a remarkable natural setting, abounding in wildlife at every turn in the creek.

At the center of this scene is Newport Farm, a former plantation and today a virtual museum of the historic and natural features of the coastal bays tidewater. The Newport Farm home, built in the early 1800s by George Purnell, stands impressively at the end of a long, tree-lined drive amid a setting that is unsurpassed along the Mid-Atlantic coast. The property is meticulously cared for by resident-owner Charles "Buddy" Jenkins, a prominent local businessman and, appropriately, the first president of Delmarva Low-Impact Tourism Experiences.

An old lime kiln still stands on Newport Farm a short distance from Newport Creek, a small tributary of Trappe Creek. Paddlers may navigate the creek by bearing west at Hayes Landing, formerly known as Newport Landing, the deep-water commercial shipping center of colonial days. In these former times, the kiln was the source for making lime used to sweeten the crop lands.

Recently, Newport Farm was also home to the last (annual) fox hunt to be run on the seaside. Seeing the hounds off on Thanksgiving Sunday was an opportunity to glimpse the expanse of this beautifully maintained property; however, the call to the hounds has now lapsed, at least temporarily.

Another feature of Newport Farm is the small lake that may be second only to the Chincoteague Wildlife refuge as a home to wintering concentrations of ducks and both snow and Canada geese. In both the early mornings and late afternoons in season, the waves of waterfowl move in and out over "Buddy's Pond," providing sport to a legion of duck hunters posted from Trappe Creek to Assateague Island.

The really good news is that Newport Farm has been placed in a permanent conservation easement by Mr. Jenkins. This is a noteworthy example of both natural and historical preservation through visionary stewardship.

Ellen Robins Whaley Patton (TP: 1991)

Mama and Papa owned several farms that had belonged in their families for generations, but Newport Farm was always the jewel in the crown. Mama had inherited the farm from Uncle Jimmy Dirickson, who also owned Sandy Point Farm (Rackliffe House property). Papa had a canning factory down there by the bay, and when the

tomatoes were being picked he rode out there (from Berlin) every day in his carriage. He had a beautiful pair of carriage horses and he really knew how to handle them. Sometimes they rode out on horseback, he and Cousin (Doctor) Zed Henry, to fox hunt. They could start the hunt by the time they got to the end of South Main Street and hunt all the way down to Newport. Then, sometimes, they would go out the other way and hunt down along Trappe Creek to Golden Quarter and over into Sinepuxent, what we used to call the Oregon Tract. 'Course all these old county roads, just like here in town, were dirt back then.

Papa and Cousin Zed had a good pack of hounds—kept up out back of our barn, but Papa always said that Cousin Zed owned half an interest in them and Cousin Zed would tell Cousin India (wife) that they all belonged to Tom Whaley. Well, you know why that was, the hounds would sometimes put up a racket you could hear all over Berlin, and it was the wives who heard all the mumblings, because nobody was going to say anything to your grandfather Tom Whaley or to Doctor Zed.

In 1916, it looked like war was coming our way. I was twelve years old and the war part didn't mean too much to me then. I do remember Papa expected to make a lot of money from the canning factory if food got tight. Well, one morning, and it was a sweltering hot summer day, sultry like the dog days we get then, he drove down to Newport Landing...I think they call it Hayes Landing now, and he didn't come back for lunch, which he usually did. I know Mama was starting to get worried, because Papa was overweight, a big man, and had diabetes. Probably high blood pressure, too. Anyway, it wasn't long before the horses and carriage rolled into the yard...the horses knew the way home blindfolded. And Papa wasn't sitting up there driving the team. Well, a search party headed down toward Newport Farm and they found him about halfway there, rolled off into a ditch. Dead. He was only 53 years old. If he had lived just a few years longer, when they had discovered insulin, he might have lived to a ripe old age. And we would have all been a lot better off, too. The war did come but Mama

> couldn't keep after the canning factory and take care of a big house full of "us chillern" plus the relatives who came and went, mostly came and stayed.
>
> She sold off Newport sometime in the twenties. I think it broke her heart, but we needed the cash and Mama was getting sick and tired of the farm tenants coming around to the house and wanting a new roof on this or that place, or needing something or another. It was like that with the Henrys, too, who owned all that land down in Sinepuxent Neck. Land rich and cash poor, they sold out like we did. And then came World War II and after that everything was worth a whole lot more money. But you just can't look back at something like that.
>
> Mama sold Newport to a Mr. Heine, who held onto it for many years and then he sold it to Buddy Jenkins about the time Pat (husband) and I started going to Florida in the winter. Well, I'm glad to hear Newport is still being kept up. So many of the old places are gone now.

Now the time has come to return to home-base in a contented frame of mind, while reflecting on the attractions of this tidewater basin. It might be well to rest the paddle for a moment, abreast of the remains of that great elm tree at Golden Quarter. Arborists have calculated that the elm began to grow into a sapling over 250 years ago, about the time Worcester County was carved out of Somerset County and the local colonists were becoming restive with their English governors. Cracks in the decaying trunk penetrate to varying stages of social development along the seaside, through wars, peace, prosperity, growth, and change. Like other great and fallen trees of prose and poem, the Golden Quarter elm may stand as a metaphor for the passing of time, and the effect on the human spirit from pondering the consequences. The dead tree is also a reminder that the special character of a region needs continual nurturing. Absentee stewardship results all too frequently in the destruction of those sacred places that make the community worth visiting and residing in.

It may still seem, at this final juncture, that the diverse elements in this chronicle have slight relation to each other, or that the connections have been stretched too far. What do

Native American Indians or old houses have to do with changing shorelines? Or hiking paths, birdwatching, and oral history to do with land development? What is there scientifically to connect the threads of social and natural history on the seaside, or anywhere else? Why is there something deep-down inside of us that craves some solid link to our heritage? Is it more than coincidence that the sounds and rhythms among the lower order of creatures are carried forward and harmonize with the wavering voices of a passing generation of mankind? For those who can scan through this dim light, the separate pieces may come together as part of the whole, much like a healthy biodiversity in the waters of the bay.

Eliminate the piping plover, the diamondback terrapin, the bald eagle, or the Delmarva Peninsula Fox Squirrel and it may be argued that the whole ecosystem will not perish. Similarly, filling in one wetland or letting a historic building collapse from neglect may not be catastrophic. Yet, there is little doubt that the system loses a certain degree of vitality when change is as irreversible as the disappearance of the Assateague Indians or an endangered species of wildlife. There is a point when the losses reach critical mass and detract from the character of the greater community. Each small loss can be another nail in the coffin.

Nothing is forever, of course. Even the Galapagos Islands, a model in ecology, are at the same time an example of evolution and change. The former insularity of the Galapagos ecosystem is now being stressed by the very forces of development spawned by its ecotourism industry. This could happen along the coastal bays, too. Market forces will probably play a heavy role in whatever happens. If the robust tourism industry begins to suffer from a blight on the natural attractions of Maryland's coastal bays and beaches, those market forces may gather to work harder in favor of heritage preservation. Now paddling the final stretch, it is also worth reflecting on the just plain pleasure derived from a fine couple of hours on the water. The tide is going out and the trip back has been tiring—a feel-good tiredness. This may be part of the contrarian nature of many who embrace the varied pursuits and ethic of outdoor adventures. The pleasure is often from the trip upstream, and contentment found in isolated water trails and quiet byways when other vacationers strive to be among the throngs on the beach.

The "unseasonable" months of the year yield some of the sweetest surprises. And evening is not just the end of the day. It's also a time to be outside—to listen to those voices in the dark, to breathe in the freshening air, and to observe. On a clear night, away from the bright resort lights, the stars are incredibly close. City dwellers can hardly believe this visibility into the night skies. It becomes a metaphysical experience.

The outcries of nature mingle with nostalgic human voices...and a Sense of Place is revealed.

Notable Homes on Trappe Creek

Golden Quarter Farm was constructed of brick c. 1761, substantially modified c. 1830, and largely reconstructed in the 1990s. The property has been carefully conserved by current owner, Sandra Frazier.

During the 1990s, local attorney Dean Jenkins commissioned the ultra-modern design of his home, bearing comparison to the renowned glass houses of Mies van der Rohe and Philip Johnson.

Photos by the author, 2004

1820 Purnell House at Newport Farm

Photo by the author

Journey's End

Standing just over a mile apart, two landmarks embody the history of Trappe Creek.

The old lime kiln (right) is located on Newport Farm within view of paddlers on Newport Creek.

Remains of the Ayres Elm at Golden Quarter Farm (left) belonged to one of the largest English Elms in Maryland: 20 feet and 1 inch in girth with a height of 90 feet and a limb-spread of 138 feet. According to legend, the tree was planted from seed in the late 1600s by an English woman. The elm grew to become a landmark along the creek, guiding ships entering the creek from Newport Bay.

Photos by the author

ACKNOWLEDGEMENTS

Credit for sticking with a balky manuscript must go to many, especially to Ron Pilling, who gave the needed encouragement and spared valuable time from his own publishing projects to help nurse this writing into a finished product. And to Ron's wife, Pat, a computer virtuoso, who provided frequent technical support. Much appreciation goes to Cathy Cooper and Kim Quillin, who waded through a very rough first draft, and to Mary Humphreys, proofreader and fact-checker extraordinaire—a marvel in her nineties; and to Connie Hall for her review of the final draft. Thanks to Tom Jones for resolving several points about the hydrodynamics of ocean currents along the Delmarva coastline.

As in the case of Ron Pilling, Dave Wilson, Director of Delmarva Low-Impact Tourism Experiences, was the right person at the right time. A journalist by trade, he gave a thumbs up and has helped enormously in securing photographs and maps showing the reader where to go and what to see and do. Both Dave Wilson and Lisa Challenger, Director of Worcester County Tourism, have been instrumental in helping secure funding for publication from those agencies and organizations recognized separately on the publication's inside cover.

This book could not have been completed without the assistance of the Assateague Island National Seashore Park staff, in particular Robert Fudge, Chief of Park Interpretation, and staffers Rachelle Daigneault and Liz Davis. In checking the accuracy of information pertaining to Assateague Island and in providing access to the Park's archives, photos, and oral histories gathered over the years, the collective assistance of the park staff has been generous. That this group exemplifies the best of public service has been my general experience over many years; our tax money well invested.

Oral histories were also extracted from the Taylor House Museum, a valuable and under-appreciated resource of local heritage. Susan Taylor, Museum Administrator, was most helpful in pointing the way to interviews pertaining to World War II memories and the recollections of life in the past century by other venerable characters in the community. Some of these interviews, as is often the case with oral histories, were completed just in time. Our thanks go to both the living and the deceased.

Pat Russells' recent involvement in transcribing oral histories for the National Park Service and the Lower Eastern Shore Heritage Committee also helped open the way to integrating selected highlights into the narrative stream of this publication. The few gleanings in this book are just the tip of the iceberg of extensive recollections that were beyond the scope here: the offshore pound fishing industry of the early 20th century; a colorful history of the gunning shanties that once speckled Assateague Island; the extensive reminiscences of since-deceased waterfowlers and decoy carvers; and stories of old Ocean City—and more, much more. Any one of these subjects would be enough for another book.

Not least, credit is given to the professional photographers who have provided contemporary perspectives of the watershed that are balanced against the old photographs. Mike Gatty's contributions are taken from his current nature photos on Assateague Island and along the coastal bays, which have been professionally exhibited as "Serenity." Andy Serrell's arresting aerial views of the watershed have been made available through courtesy of the Maryland Coastal Bays Program. Patrick Henry's paintings and photo studies of the coastal bays are examples in themselves of heritage preservation.

ADDENDUM: SOME ECO-DO'S AND DON'TS

LEAVE NO FOOTPRINTS: A principal ethic of ecotourism is recreation without diminishing the natural and historic resources of the area. Create no litter. Enjoy, and leave it as before.

SUPPORT ORGANIZATIONS AND OPERATORS that subscribe to the ethic of Delmarva's Low-Impact Tourism Experiences (D-LITE) and work to preserve the coastal watershed.

CHOOSE A QUIET DAY ON THE WATER: Enjoy a canoe trip or a sail down the bays. Listen to and reflect on the sounds of Nature.

KEEP THE BAY WATERS CLEAN by avoiding spills of oil or gas. Toss nothing overboard.

LEAVE CAMP AND RECREATION SITES PICKED UP: Put trash in bins if available; in primitive sites, pack it out. Use recycle stations, where available.

MAINTAIN PETS UNDER CONTROL AT ALL TIMES: Wandering pets can attack wildlife; lost pets that become feral are a major problem.

DON'T FEED THE WILDLIFE: Assateague ponies can be meddlesome. Sea gull populations are already exploding, which leads to their predation on threatened and endangered turtle and bird eggs and hatchlings.

KNOW THE SENSITIVE OR PROHIBITED AREAS and tread accordingly. Avoid piping plover and other shorebird nesting areas in season. Consult recent maps and guidelines published by the Maryland Department of Natural Resources and Assateague Island park entities.

BE GUIDED BY FISHING, CRABBING, AND CLAMMING REGULATIONS if engaged in recreational fishing activities. Regulations are available at local tackle shops.

ON GATHERING WILD FOODS: Always ask permission from the appropriate public or private authority.

ASK PERMISSION TO ENTER PRIVATE PROPERTY whether to hike, bird-watch, or visit a historic structure.

RESPECT HISTORIC SITES and do not remove relics from public or private property without permission. Native American relics should normally be left in place.

PRIMARY REFERENCES

American Guide Series. *Maryland: A Guide to the Old Line State.* Compiled by workers of the Writers' Program of the Work Projects Administration in the State of Maryland, Sponsored by Herbert R. O'Connor, Governor of Maryland. Oxford University Press, NY, 1940.

Bearss, Ewin C. *General Background Study and Historical Base Map, Assateague Island National Seashore.* Division of History, Office of Archeology and Historic Preservation, National Park Service, U. S. Department of the Interior, 1968.

Birindelli, Ben. *The 200 Year Legacy of Stephen Decatur 1798-1998.* Hallmark Publishing Company, Gloucester Point, VA, 1998.

Carey. George G. *Maryland Folklore and Folklife.* Tidewater Publishers, Centreville, MD, 1970.

Colombe, Deborah A. *The Seaside Naturalist.* Simon & Schuster, Fireside Edition, 1992.

Custer, Jay F. *Prehistoric Cultures of the Delmarva Peninsula: An Archaelogical Study.* Univ. Of Delaware Press, Newark, DE, 1989.

DeVincent-Hayes, Nan, and Bo Bennett. *Chincoteague and Assateague Islands: Images of America.* Arcadia Publishing, Charleston, SC, 2000.

Dryden, Ruth T. *Land Records of Worcester County, Maryland, 1666-1810.* San Diego, CA. Printed privately 1987.

Environmental Protection Agency (United States EPA). "How Will Climate Change Affect the Mid-Atlantic Region?". EPA/903/F-00/002, June 2001.

Fisher, Allan. *Daytrips in Delmarva.* Rambler Books, Baltimore, 1998.

Forman, Henry Chandlee. *Tidewater Maryland Architecture and Gardens.* Bonanza Books, a division of Crown Publishers, by arrangement with the Architectural Book Publishing Company, 1956.

Gibbons, Euell. *Stalking the Blue-Eyed Scallop.* David McKay Company, NY, 1964.

Heilner, Van Campen, and Frank Stick. *The Call of the Surf.* Doubleday, Page & Company. 1920.

Himes, Sharon. *Cavalier's Adventure: The Story of Henry Norwood.* Arcadia Productions, Princess Anne, MD, 2000.

Hurley, George and Suzanne. *Shipwrecks and Rescues Along the Barrier Islands of Delaware, Maryland, and Virginia.* The Conning Company, Norfolk/Virginia Beach, 1984

Jacob, John E., Janet Carter, and Ellis Wainwright. *Worcester County: Postcard History Series.* Arcadia Publishing, Charleston, SC, 2000.

Kenny, Hamill. *The Origin and Meaning of the Indian Place Names of Maryland.* Waverly Press, Baltimore, 1961.

National Park Service. *A Guide to Assateague Island National Seashore: Assateague Island.* Handbook 106, U.S. Department of the Interior, 1980.

Perry, Bill. *The Life of Assateague: A guide to three Nature Trails in Assateague National Seashore.* Eastern National in cooperation with the National Park Service, 1999.

Porter, Frank W. *Indians in Maryland and Delaware, A Critical Bibliography.* Indiana University Press, Bloomington and London, 1979.

Roundtree, Helen C. and Thomas E. Davidson. *Eastern Shore Indians of Virginia and Maryland.* University Press of Virginia, Charlottesville, 1997.

Stout, Gardner D., Peter Matthiessen, Robert Clem, and Ralph Palmer. *The Shorebirds of North America.* The Viking Press, New York, 1967.

Touart, Paul Baker. *Along the Seaboard Side: The Architectural History of Worcester County, Maryland.* By Worcester County, Snow Hill, MD. 1994..

Truitt, Reginald V. *Assateague...The Place Across.* Natural Resources Institute, University of Maryland, Educational Series No. 90, 1971.

Truitt, Reginald V. *High Winds...High Tides: A Chronicle of Maryland's Coastal Hurricanes.* National Resources Institute, University of Maryland, Educational Series No. 77, 1968.

Truitt, Reginald V. and Millard G. Les Callette. *Worcester County: Maryland's Arcadia.* Worcester County Historical Society, Snow Hill, MD, 1977.

Vallandigham, Edward Noble. *Delaware and The Eastern Shore.* J. B. Lippincott Company, Philadelphia, 1922.

Whaley Papers 1680-2001. Private Library of Thomas Patton. Unpublished Essays, Illustrations, photographs, and genealogies of early Seaside families: Whaley, Henry, Purnell, Robins, and Dirickson.

ADDITIONAL INFORMATION

Tourism booklets and pamphlets are widely available at information centers, including Assateague Island National Seashore Visitor Center and the Worcester County Office of Tourism (partial listing below):

Assateague Island, A Guide to Assateague Island National Seashore, Maryland and Virginia Division of Publications, National Park Service, U.S. Department of the Interior.

Assateague Island Water Trails. Exploring Coastal Bay & Salt Marsh Flats of Assateague Island.

Barrier Island Handbook, Dr. Stephen P. Leatherman (U. Of Maryland, 1988).

Birdwatcher's Guide to Delmarva. Delmarva Advisory Council's Atlantic Flyway Byway Consortium. 1999.

Maryland Coastal Bays Program, Today's Treasures for Tomorrow, An Environmental Report on Maryland's Coastal Bays. Maryland Department of Natural Resources, *MCBP 97-01.*

Pamphlets:

"Birdwatching in Worcester County, MD"

"Birdwatcher's Checklist, Worcester County, MD"

"Assateague Island SEASHELLS"

"Assateague Island MAMMALS"

"The Life of Assateague, A Guide to Three Nature Trails in Assateague Island National Seashore"

"Nature Trails in Worcester County, Maryland"

"Great Delmarva Bicycling Trail"

"Sinepuxent Bay Water Trails"

"Lower Eastern Shore Maryland: A Historic Cultural Crossroad"